Product Marketing Effective Go To Market Strategy

SADANAND PUJARI

Published by SADANAND PUJARI, 2023.

Table of Contents

Copyright

Product Marketing Effective Go To Market Strategy

First Edition: Dec 2023

Book Design by **SADANAND PUJARI**

About

Welcome to Product Marketing: Effective Go-To-Market Strategy

The best products can still lose in the marketplace. Why? They are beaten by products with stronger product marketing. Good product marketing is the difference between "also-ran" products versus products that lead. And yet, product marketing is widely misunderstood. Although it includes segmenting customers, positioning your product, creating product collateral, and supporting sales teams, great product marketing achieves much more. It directs the best way to bring your product to market. It shapes what the world thinks about your product and category. It inspires others to tell your product's story.

Product success starts with making the right strategic decisions. But the challenge for many product teams is that they are often so preoccupied with the tactics that they no longer see the forest for the trees.

This Book will help you proactively create a winning product strategy and an actionable product roadmap using a wide range of proven tools and techniques.

So Let's Do This! Enroll now and sharpen your product strategy skills. See you on the inside!

Introduction

Coca Cola is one of the world's most successful consumer products, yet the typical customer only buys it once or twice per year. Most business to business marketers are really only interested in generating short term results. Yet only 5% of business to business buyers are even remotely considering buying this corner. These bizarre findings teach us something about product marketing. It's that product marketing is not intuitive. It's full of surprises that go against conventional marketing wisdom.

That's why this Book is needed. Welcome to become a product marketing manager. I was a vice president of marketing for Google Accelerator Startup. I was a global product marketing manager for Sony PlayStation. I was a senior product marketing manager in Silicon Valley, and I was a product marketing manager for a Google venture startup. I've done product marketing consulting for countless companies of all sizes in business to consumer and business to business.

I received my MBA in marketing from Philip Cutler's Kellogg School of Management, the number one ranked business school for marketing in the United States. I taught college level marketing and I published two product marketing books. My general philosophy guiding this Book is that you either go big or you go back to selling services. Unlike marketing, something like an agency or a professional service firm, product marketing is fundamentally about scale. Economies of scale and market share will be even the best targeting, messaging and positioning. Let's get started.

Product Positioning Mistakes

We're going to talk about a number of critical misunderstandings that product marketing managers have with respect to positioning. So one of the first mistakes is believing that emotional positioning is better than rational or functional positioning. This simply isn't true. We have research from McKinsey, for example, showing that positioning around functional benefits or things like product features tend to generate stronger word of mouth than positioning around emotions.

And this is even true when we're talking about consumer products like cosmetics, where you would think that emotional positioning would be better now. My general view on this is that high level positioning is not necessarily better than low level positioning. And what I mean here is we're talking about the value ladder. So at the bottom you have technical features and at the top you have kind of emotions or in the business to business space, it'd be something like helping profitability versus at the bottom. It might be something like connecting two items.

Things like that do not make the assumption that higher level benefits or high level positioning is superior than functional level positioning. Okay. Another critical misunderstanding is believing that positioning is just product positioning. So there's different types of positioning. Product positioning tends to be more rational. The reason it's more rational is because when people are evaluating products, it is because they want to make a decision to trial the product, to do a pilot of the product to purchase the product. Okay. But then there's also brand positioning, which is separate.

Brand positioning tends to be more emotional. It tends to be more focused on the long term, and it isn't necessarily based around rational things because it's not trying to get people to make a rational decision. It's trying to get people to remember your brand and associate it with some sort of product category or some sort of purchase decision, but not in a precise analytical way, more in kind of a broad psychological way. So you can position your product and your brand differently. And there tends to be a split there between rational and emotional, but that's not universally true. Now, you also have services which may be supplementing or separate from the product that you're selling. You can position the services differently. Okay.

Now one of the more common mistakes that I see is with advertising. So your advertisement can take positioning that is different from your product and that is different from your brand. The reason is because an individual advertisement needs to deliver a single message a lot of the time because it can be too overwhelming to deliver an ad that talks about the entirety of the product, the entirety of the solution, the entirety of the value proposition. So when an ad could just talk about one benefit, one feature, one job to be done, one use case, you can also have a campaign that is positioned differently from your product, your brand, etcetera. So the campaign, for example, could talk about one benefit and then each individual ad talks about the features or the reasons to believe that benefit, or you could have the reverse where you're talking about one feature and the benefits that come from that.

Now, the other critical thing to understand is that the positioning can be different based on who you're targeting. So partners, for example, are going to care about things that are different from prospective customers. So prospective partners, you may position around certain types of value. Maybe the positioning is more around financial value reimbursements or strategic value that has very little to do with revenue. You can also position your product differently and your advertisements, your messages or emails, etcetera differently based on the key personas that you're targeting or the individuals within companies for the different sub segments of your target customer.

Another critical misunderstanding is believing that positioning is strategy. Now, this is a little bit of a linguistic debate, but for the sake of consistency, I would say that strategy is choosing target markets that you're going to participate in and how you create value in those target markets, which is for customers, for partners and for your own company. So it's the target market and the value proposition positioning is more tactical. I wouldn't say it's completely tactical because you're making big trade off decisions when it comes to your messaging and stuff, but it's not as strategic as your value proposition.

Basically, positioning is deciding what gets emphasized in your messaging in specific contexts, and those contexts are going to vary and there's going to be various gradients where you're going to apply those positionings based on who you're targeting and whether you're talking about product positioning, brand positioning or service positioning.

Dyson Product Marketing Example

Brand vs Product Marketing Example Unlike brand marketing, product marketing caters more to people who are "in-market" and will therefore make a purchase decision soon. In order to make a purchase decision, they need lots of information! "The more you tell, the more you sell!" I'm in the market for a cordless vacuum. The detail I need is the charging mechanism. I want to know that it can be charged in a dock without needing to be plugged in. This is a nuance that brand marketers would ignore, but product marketers must point out to secure a sale from me.

I simply will not buy a vacuum without this feature. You see: product marketing is not just about finding ONE thing to position your product around. It requires an annoyingly high degree of product detail. This is especially true when marketing to engineers. Most product listings fail to talk about the charging experience at all, but a select few will number out each and every key component and feature, often in excruciating detail. Poor product marketers talk excessively about one high-level benefit without giving adequate details to make that benefit believable or even to meet the most basic feature requirements.

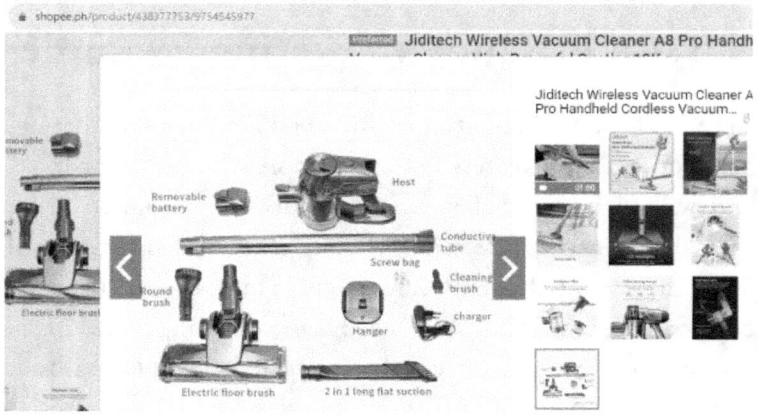

Step 1: Brand marketing to stay top-of-mind whenever a customer goes in market in the future Step 2: Prospect goes in market with a bias towards familiar brands Step 3: Prospect evaluates & eliminates products based on details/requirements Step 4: Purchase Dyson does an excellent job both promoting its luxury brand AND promoting the granular details of each product.

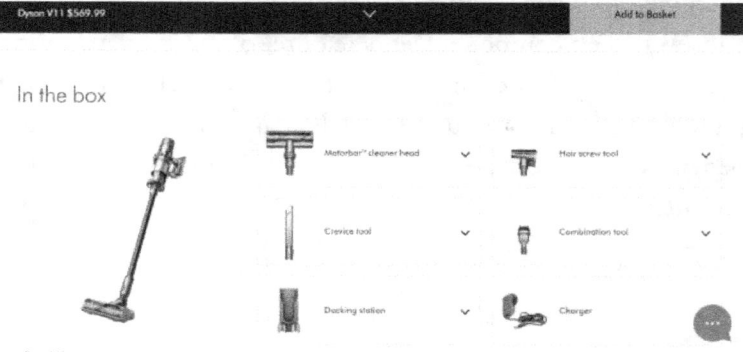

In the next chapter I explain why simply listing all the features & benefits is not adequate. You do have to figure out what buyers really want and then provide adequate detail to prove you can deliver on your promise. The key is understanding how you create value.

Key B2B Marketing Notes

I want to give you a recent example of why I think it is a bad idea to simply list a series of benefits and features and really kind of focus on the key thing. Now, in this case, it's actually not that bad because there are three points of difference that this person is highlighting. In a lot of cases, they're using ten. But even here, I don't think it's the best approach. So I'm engaging in this LinkedIn conversation with someone and I'm asking them, Well, okay, so your product, why isn't it different from what I'm doing now? And he says, Well, I will give you three reasons.

First, and then the name of the product that I've censored here gives you the possibility to scale by searching new prospects worldwide. Second, you will get premium support, and third, you will get it for free to check all the advantages. Now, I don't really care about the last two points. Premium support. Okay, well, I don't even I don't even know if I need this product at all. The support is kind of this ten gentle thing. It's not core to the value of the product.

Now, with some products, maybe support is hugely important, but it isn't for this. This is an email tool and Of course I'm satisfied with the support I'm getting from the current product. And if I wasn't, perhaps I would have switched already. You'll get it for free. Well, I don't really care to get something for free if I don't even know if I like it or need it. In any case, almost every product that I want to try is going to have some sort of free trial option anyway. So both of these are irrelevant. The only one that's really relevant is this first point about scaling by searching for new prospects worldwide.

So I think this person could have benefitted by just focusing on this one thing, but getting more specific, I mean, scale, every product basically helps you scale, searching new prospects worldwide. Why? I mean, every prospecting tool is going to hopefully provide worldwide options or that's not really a concern that I have, that it won't be global because I, I just assume that's the case with most products these days. So really what I feel this person could have done was just give more detail about this particular point and then that would be more compelling than trying to list out everything, because these are really, in my mind, either points of irrelevance or points of parity with competing solutions. So this brings me to another point, which is that a lot of things that companies think or think are points of difference may just be points of parody.

They're just not all different from what competing solutions offer, what your competitors offer, and highlighting them to the prospect is just kind of they don't care. They're not going to be listening because they're just like, well, you know, Joe Blow's product does the same thing. Now, a key thing that you may want to do is change the frame of reference. So when they're comparing you to competitors, they're going to be looking at things like points of difference points or parity points of irrelevance. But the other thing that they're going to be doing is that they may have some sort of KPI in mind. So an example that James Anderson points out here, when you're selling something like paint is the buyer may be looking at the price per leader, but you can change the reference and you can say, you know what, let's not let's not have a discussion about price per leader.

Let's have a discussion about the outcome you want, which is price per code at home so you can change the conversation and make yourself more competitive based on how you frame the decision making and focusing it on outcomes that you're better at achieving rather than kind of a pure price or a traditional method of comparison. Another key thing that you need to do is to think about how your value stack will kind of fit the series of benefits, use cases, savings, and additional profits that you contribute to the needs of individuals or the most important people in the decision making process. So I'm giving the example here where we have a value stack on the left and we have the personas that we're targeting on the right. So on the left we have integrated X and Y, saves X dollars per unit, speeds up Y and automates Z. So in this case, it may be that the CEO really values saving money and speeding up.

Where is the director of t i.t. Values the integration and then the marketing manager values speeding and automated. So when you do something like send direct mail, call emails, etc. to the marketing manager, you should focus on these key benefits. And then when you message the CEO, focus on other ones. So personas, specific targeting and messaging is going to make your marketing much more effective. A lot of success in business. In business marketing is going to stem from collaboration and analysis related to the sales team. And one of the key things is that sales often don't follow up with leads. Now, often that's because the leads are bad quality and they just come from ebook downloads or something useless like that. Or it could just be that there's a poor handoff to the sales team.

And one of the ways you fix that is with operations where you're optimizing, for example, the information that's being transferred from lead forms to the sales force notes. So the sales team can follow up appropriately and relevantly and talk to the customer where they're at, rather than sort of assuming a certain level of awareness that they don't have. Another important thing is that you should follow up fast. Now, I've heard recently in the business to business marketing sphere this idea that this is outdated. I disagree. I think speed of follow up is important. Now, maybe it's less important when you're dealing with certain types of strategic purchases when you only have a couple of key competitors.

But for a lot of business to business products, following up fast is going to be incredibly important, especially when what happens is there's some sort of key trigger event where somebody needs a quick solution, and that's the time when they have availability to discuss it. One way, one way to resolve that is, is to track the follow up time and use that as a KPI. Using data from Salesforce or whatever your CRM is. Okay. Another thing to think about, and this is something that business to business marketers sometimes get wrong is you need to consider the next best alternative.

Now, the next best alternative often is not what you think. So a lot of people think they're competing against Excel spreadsheets and they're like, Oh, okay, well, we can crush Excel spreadsheets if you're selling software or you may sort of put yourself against some sort of legacy product that really isn't the next best alternative because the prospect is looking to get away from Excel. They're looking to get away from some old machinery they're using. So that means they're probably looking at competitors.

So you're up against tougher competition than you think. It's not going to be some basic free solution. They're going to be comparing you to other people that have much more value to offer. Now, the other thing to think about is that your product category is not always going to be the next best alternative. It could be something like, Well, why don't we just hire somebody to do that? Or Why don't we just outsource and get it done manually? Maybe we don't need machinery, maybe we don't need automation. Maybe we don't need software to do this. We can just get somebody to do it. So you can do your research, talk to prospects, see what they say, and try to get honest opinions.

Because if you suggest, Oh, we have this product to do this, they might just be like, Well, I could just pay somebody in the Philippines X dollars per hour to do it. I don't need machinery to do that. I don't need automation. Another thing that people often get hung up on is the idea that they're trying to increase the profitability of a specific purchase or a specific order. But as you start to become more advanced, you need to think about customer lifetime value and start tracking that over time, because ultimately that's what you're tracking now. People that really get this are people that have platforms. So for example, Richie Burrows with Business to Business Auctioning online, they're going to think about the overall profitability of the system and perhaps less obsessed over profitability of individual orders because business to business customers are sticky and they're going to be absorbed. They're going to have recurring business.

They may be locked into contracts for years. So you need to think about overall customer lifetime value, not just at the granularity of specific orders and specific products. Now what I just said about business to business customers being sticky or captive in the terminology of Bruce Greenwald, this is a difficult challenge to overcome. But one way you can do it is you provide prospects, incentives to try your product and incentives to switch your product. So I've seen a lot of success getting business to business buyers to try products by just paying them. You know, here's $200 or here is a $100 Amazon gift card.

We just want you to sit through a demo of a product. Hear what we have to say. And they may not even ask for the incentive at the end of it, because they just see there's so much value and that they don't care about getting that money. But it's certainly effective at generating pipelines. Now, the other thing is incentives to switch. So I'll give you an example here often. One of the reasons people may not be considering buying your product is because they have a long term contract with a competitor. So maybe they're on a three year contract. They're only two years in. Well, you can offer to buy the remainder of the contract and that lubricates this resistance to switching. You can also just pay them money and say, you know, well, we'll just pay you or we'll give you the first six months free. Just sign the contract for one year. Okay.

Now, in business to business, what I often see is segmentation approached wrong. Now, the key thing that I often see that's wrong is personal identification. And they're using variables that are just irrelevant. So Suzy, she's 47, she's a director of marketing. She has a dog. You know, these demographic details, they're colorful and cute, but they don't matter. What matters is okay, well, the job title didn't matter. Marketing Director But most importantly are going to be things like how are they using the product, what are the benefits they're looking for, etc.. So traditional segmentation I'm not saying it's wrong would be former graphic demographic types of things, size of company and that may be relevant but it's really relevant when it's correlated with more progressive types of segmentation and some examples I'm demonstrating below. So the first is application. How are they applying the product?

How are they using it? That's going to be one of the most important things. And what you may find is there's actually overlap. It may be that medium size companies are using the product in the same way that large companies are. So that separation between medium and large may not be relevant for you. Also capabilities. What are those companies capable of so large? Sophisticated companies may not care for your support. They have internal resources to do it, but smaller companies may value it a lot more or certain industries may value it more. So if you sell to the tech industry, maybe they don't need a lot of your technical acumen, but perhaps industrial companies may value it a lot more. And that means that that segment should receive a lot of that messaging about how you're going to handhold them through the technical capabilities.

Another thing is to segment based on the usage situation. So are people using this for access or are they using it for Y? And some of those things may surprise you. They may not be the main use situation that you had in mind when first marketing the product. But when you actually talk to customers and look at data, you'll realize something different. So for example, one thing that I realized was that large companies that a company I was working for really were not using our inventory capabilities. The reason was because they had dedicated systems to track inventory and this was contrary to what we expected. So they used this situation for them, had more to do with accounting, less in terms of inventory.

Now the other segmentation you can do is based on profit contribution. So there are going to be customers who contribute a lot more to profit. And what you can do is you can do things like create lookalike audiences on Facebook targeting and say, hey, go find me other people like this. And hopefully there will be bigger contributions to profit in the future. Okay. Two key concepts that I need to talk about that a lot of people miss in business to business versus value drains. The value drains are things where they're very costly things for you to provide, but they don't actually provide a lot of value. So for example, often you start with some sort of core product and that's how your business became successful.

And then you start adding on things to your core product to kind of enhance it, but the customer doesn't really use it, and you can look at data. So you might go into power by and see, okay, are people using your product? Or you might do research, just go to the customer's plant and see how they're using your product. And you may realize, okay, they're not really using this thing. We add it or they're not really using the support, the 24 hour support that we have at it. But you actually invested a lot of resources in being able to provide it and then realizing that, hey, this isn't actually creating a lot of value. And often this means you just need a kind of reverse strategy and stick to what you're actually good at, which is the core offering. So that was a value drain.

Now there's something that's even worse and this is a valve leak. And these are things that actually increase the costs of your customers to do business. And these are things that often you actually think are key benefits, key points of difference that make your product better. They actually make it worse. And I'm going to give you an example. From my experience, we had perhaps the most sophisticated technology in our competitive space. And what that meant was that we were able to transfer all types of granular data in real time. So we had order specific technicalities, we had line cost items, we had all this information.

We were able to just constantly integrate between systems. And that sounds like a benefit, right? The more the more detailed the technicalities, the faster a story, the quicker you were able to get that information, the better. But when I was doing research and the way I did research was I studied the influencers. So the professionals that influence our customers, you know, looking at their videos, looking at how they review different business to business solutions. One thing that they were concerned about was that this actually overloads the servers. It's too much data, too fast, and much more than the customers would ever need. So this thing that we thought was a fundamental advantage of the product was actually a disadvantage.

It was actually hurting customers, it was providing negative value. It was a valve leak. And you'd be surprised at how many large enterprise companies that you think would have all of this figured out don't. And they're actually pushing things that destroy value for customers.

Budgeting

The real secret to going big with your marketing is when you start to think of yourself like a portfolio manager. So, for example, in the investment world, managers may be allocating budgets towards large companies, towards high growth potential companies. They might throw in some bonds, they have a smorgasbord of different investments that they're playing with. And the idea is let's get the allocation right. The problem that I see with a lot of marketers is they don't really think like portfolio managers. They're more interested in figuring out what channels best, how do I fully optimize a given channel?

And generally there's heavy, heavy emphasis on the bottom of the funnel where they're just trying to either generate leads in business to business, particularly marketing qualified leads, or they're trying to generate sales when they're doing something like business to consumer e-commerce. But sophisticated marketing doesn't work like that. That's not how you achieve economies of scale. It's not how you achieve efficiency. You achieve those things by doing integrated marketing communications. And integrated marketing communications means that you need to allocate time, resources and budget towards each stage of the funnel and then synergize together.

You're able to get the outcomes that you want, which is going to be things like pipeline revenue and B2B or sales, B2C, customer acquisition, user acquisition, etc.. So generally speaking, based on empirical research, the optimal allocation of your budget is going to be around 50% top of funnel and 50% bottom of funnel. Now I'd like to break this down further and I have the top of the funnel, the middle of the funnel in the bottom of the funnel. And then if you want to get even more granular, these are the stages of awareness that I want to appeal to at each stage of the funnel. So at the very top we have brand- unaware people, people that aren't familiar with your logo, they're not familiar with their brand name. So what you should be doing is you should be taking a percentage of your budget and allocating it purely towards brand awareness, and you're not going to measure success based on sales, clicks, etc..

You're going to be measuring it based on things like Reach, brand recall, brand awareness, brand fame. Are people associating your brand with the buying situation or with the trigger event? So perhaps if they get sued, do they think of using your legal software, for example, or if they have a new website, do they think about using your e-commerce integration or your live chat? So the way that you measure success of brand awareness is often not that easy. It might involve things like survey research or potentially qualitative interviews, talking to people that visit your website, things like that. So behavioral metrics aren't necessarily that definitive when you're dealing with the top of the funnel. So because things are unclear because it's a bit of WiFi coffee, that's why a lot of product marketing managers don't bother doing it at all.

But you do need to do it and you should be allocating a large budget towards it. Now the second stage is a problem for aware people. So these are people that are not aware that the problem that you solve, that your product solves, is actually worth prioritizing, it's worth paying attention to. So you need to spend marketing convincing them that that problem needs to be focused on and it needs to be prioritized over other problems. And you can do things like using research to do that.

Now, one of the reasons that I have a brand on Aware at the far left here is because when you're doing brand marketing, pure brand marketing, and I'm talking about marketing, the brand that's pegged to the product separate from the product itself. So there's the product which has its features, and then there's the brand which creates value over and above the features of the product. And that's something that you kind of slap on as a label. So that's going to be things like your mascot, your logo, your brand name, etc.. So there's this brand marketing as an asset that needs to be treated differently.

Now, one of the reasons that is very different from these other stages, generally speaking, is because brand marketing is something that you do for the long term. And long term marketing often revolves more around things like emotions and maybe loose affiliations with things. Whereas when you're marketing something like your product, it tends to be much more straightforward and rational. Talking about the justification for buying you, talking about specific use cases, etc. As we move into the middle of the funnel, there are people that need to be convinced that whatever product category you're in is something that they need to engage in to solve their problems. So for example, if you're a live chat plug-in, you need to convince them that live chat is the solution to their problem, not necessarily your product or your specific brand, but just the category in general.

For example, I was marketing dictation software for veterinarians, and because this was fairly new that a lot of veterinarians don't use dictation software, the marketing is really about selling. Dictation itself, the virtues of dictation. It's kind of minor as to what specific product or brand is being pegged to that message at that point. Now, next, what does matter is your specific product, how it's different, how it creates value over and above the competition, why they should choose you specifically and making sure that people actually remember your specific product.

Now, one of the big problems I see when you go to websites that product marketing managers have worked on is the website is 100% focused on getting the conversion like a demo request, a free trial, sign up, a free consultation, etc.. But really what ends up happening is 70% of those leads, according to Dr. James Anderson, basically get ignored or thrown out by the sales team. So what's happening here? I think one of the big things that's happening is these people are being pressured or cajoled into signing up for demo requests, but they haven't even really gotten any product education. So one area where I think product marketing managers could improve is using the website as an education tool, less as a conversion tool so that we have some asset that is focused on creating product awareness, product education.

Now, moving into the bottom of the funnel, we have people that are free offer unaware. So your free offer is like your free trial, your demo, your consultation, etc.. Now, a lot of people do focus here and they focus here too much. One of the reasons they focus here too much, I believe, is because it's not really scalable. There are only so many people that are willing to show up to a sales meeting to contact you, to engage one on one with the salesperson, or in the case of e-commerce or business consumers, maybe sign up to get coupons or something like that. So in this case, there are things you can do that can optimize your marketing that a lot of people don't. So for example, you can incentivize people to show up to meetings.

And despite what a lot of people might say, this is actually very effective and there's tons of case studies to show that you can generate million dollars plus by doing campaigns promoting things like gift cards or giving people money to show up to something like a demo. Now, the last stage here we have paid off or on Aware, so people that need to be educated about your contract terms, they need to be convinced to pull the trigger. There needs to be some sense of urgency to get them to sign up for your product and not competing products. Now, fundamentally, this is where sales plays a role, but there is a role in marketing. So here what we're doing is we're helping with sales enablement, we're helping with battle decks, we're helping by doing competitive comparisons, and we're helping by always doing marketing.

So always marketing to people, even before they become customers, even when they're in this sort of bottom of the funnel stage. Familiarity with your brand and your product is really going to help seal the deal. So the big decision you really need to make is allocating a budget to each of these stages or maybe using different stages. That's fine. But the point is that you need to commit to putting the budget towards the top of the funnel, the middle of the funnel, not just the bottom of the funnel. And you need to do that from the get go because if you don't make that commitment from the get go, what's going to happen is you're going to start looking at the data and you may have ran a campaign that was designed just to create brand awareness, but then you're like, Oh, it's not getting many clicks, it's not getting many purchases.

Let's kind of pause that campaign and put more budget here. That's the wrong way to do it. You need to commit to doing things that are purely about education, purely about brand awareness, purely about things that are going to set the stage for more scalable bottom of funnel conversions ultimately down the road and down the road. I mean, in six plus months, not just focused on what's going to happen to meet quota this month.

Profit

Product To Market - Profit I want to walk you through a very basic formula for profit. This is important because it will help you sell your marketing initiatives internally and help you prioritize what you should be working on. It's really quite simple. Profit equals revenue minus expenses. But we can expand this to understand what drives revenue and what drives expenses. So now we have profit equals average price times quantity minus average cost times quantity.

I prefer the simpler version of this. In other words price minus cost times quantity. So you see there are really only three ways to increase profit: change the price, change the cost or change the quantity sold. It's really that simple. Everything you do as a marketer can be tied back to these three simple things that drive profit. Let's elaborate. As a marketer you are usually focused on generating more revenue. Marketers aren't interested in the cost side of the equation. So to increase revenue there are two approaches: you can either sell more or you can raise prices. Raising prices is a pretty simple task but selling more is a bit more complicated to sell more. You can either get more customers, increase the frequency of transactions or increase the size of transactions.

All of these help you some more and hence increase revenue. If we go a layer deeper there are actually two ways to get more customers. You can acquire more or you can increase retention so that more customers stay either of these will increase your customer base. So this is basically a summary of what you're trying to do as a marker to increase revenue in all these various ways whatever decisions you make whether it's running a TV campaign or shifting focus to a different target customer. You need to tie it back to one or more of these drivers. Now I'd like to go even more advanced with this analysis because you see the purpose of a company is not to generate as much profit as possible.

It is to have a high return on investment. In other words a company's purpose is to be efficient at generating profit, not simply to generate as much profit as possible. Let me explain. Let's say your company has a ton of cash and millions of dollars. The company could invest it in the stock market and get a 10 percent return on that cash. It could also give it back to shareholders and let them spend it. Maybe they could invest about 11 percent in return. The third option is that the company could take that money and invest it back in the company itself. But what if investing back in the company itself would only generate a 5 percent return. Well that's awful because the company would have been better off investing in the stock market or simply giving the money back to shareholders.

The company cannot be efficient at generating profit in this situation. So it shouldn't focus on generating profit. It should instead allocate money outside the company. That may lead to less profit for the company but it leads to a better return for the shareholders of the company. There is one situation where companies are generating profit. This is where the return on capital is greater than the cost of capital. In other words this is where the company has a competitive advantage and there are basically just two types of competitive advantage: customer captivity and economies of scale. So as an advanced marketer you're interested in a couple of things.

The first is generating profit which usually boils down to increasing revenue. The second is maintaining focus where competitive advantages exist. So for example acquiring customers who are captive and ensuring that economies of scale are achieved in marketing efforts advanced marketing doesn't just mean spending money. So long as a profit is generated advance marketing is about investing in areas where competitive advantages exist and building those competitive advantages.

The Big Mistake in B2B

Product Marketing that People Keep Making One of the biggest and most common mistakes in B2B product marketing is failing to ask this critical question: "Am I selling a strategic or non-strategic purchase?" Without realizing it, most people market their products as strategic purchases because they're not even aware that the question above needs to be asked.

This leads to a number of critical marketing errors: Spending way too much time trying to differentiate your product from competitors when customers just don't care Failure to generate pipeline because marketing-captured leads aren't converting into demo requests, free trials, and sales calls Failure to close opportunities because Sales is pushing strategic attributes that are irrelevant Over-emphasis on benefits when customers care more about features To determine if your product is a strategic purchase, ask yourself: "Does my product help customers differentiate their product to their customers?" Reference: James Anderson, PhD JungleScout, for example, is a strategic purchase because it helps Amazon sellers make critical strategic decisions about what new products to add to their portfolios.

Those product offerings differentiate Amazon sellers from one another. SnapEngage, on the other hand, is a non-strategic purchase. It is a live-chat plugin for your website that doesn't fundamentally change how you differentiate yourself to customers. When you are marketing a non-strategic purchase, you shouldn't waste time on differentiation and making unnecessary price concessions[1].

Instead, focus on elements that will help lubricate the sales process, such as: Risk-free cancellations with a money-back guarantee Free onboarding with custom configurations Access to senior consultants If you fail to ask whether your product is a strategic purchase, your positioning, sales enablement, and demand generation will all miss the mark.

---

1. https://hbr.org/2014/03/tiebreaker-selling

PART 1 : Competitive Analysis

Competitive analysis. Competitive analysis is an important role for product marketing managers. That's because product managers are often too wrapped up in critical day to day operations. They don't have time to analyze the competitive environment. The challenge with competitive analysis is that you can do it forever. There's no limit to the level of detail. For that reason, I have three approaches to help narrow your analysis. This will help you prioritize the most important aspects of the analysis. The first approach is what I call the specific purpose analysis.

The second focuses on competitive advantage, and the third starts with marketing strategy and ends with marketing tactics. Let's start with the first approach for a specific purpose. Here you narrow your analysis to the specific purpose for which you were doing it. In this way, you skip all strategies and tactics that are irrelevant to the decision you are trying to arrive at.

For example, let's say you were trying to figure out how to optimize your login experience. You might look at Google's login. Note the text call to action colors and user flow. You can then look at other competitors of yours. You aren't interested in dissecting entire strategies. You were just looking at logins for your competitors. You can then document certain aspects in a table, for example, the number of login fields required.

PART 2 : Competitive Analysis

Now let's consider the competitive advantage approach. My process is based on the book Competition Demystified. This is one of the best business books ever written. It discusses the fundamental basis of a company's success. There are essentially two types of competitive advantage. The first is economies of scale. The second is customer captivity. Note that I haven't included brands, advertising or even strategic buzzwords such as value propositions or target markets. Competitive advantage is mostly based on economies of scale and customer captivity. I'll explain each of these in detail.

Economies of scale enable a company to lower its cost as it gets bigger. Let me give you an example. Let's say a company has a lot of fixed costs in a factory. As it gets more and more customers, it is able to spend its fixed costs and spread those costs across each of its customers. It's kind of like each customer shares a smaller and smaller piece of the fixed costs. And as more customers are added, the incremental cost gets smaller and smaller. As a side note, economies of scale usually break down at a certain size, so there is a limit.

In analyzing competitors, there are many different ways to estimate scale. One is using a website such as Web.com or Spyfu. Here you can estimate the amount of traffic your competitors are getting and how much money they are spending on specific keywords. You could also look to social media for the number of followers that your competitors have.

Here you can see that Sephora has nearly 17 million followers. Another approach is to use surveys to gauge brand awareness.

Brand awareness can be measured in different ways. One approach would be to get a random sample of customers and ask them What shoe companies can you name? If 50% of people name your competitor, then the brand awareness is 50%. This is called unaided awareness because you left the question open ended. It didn't supply the customers with brand names beforehand. With aided brand awareness, you might give a list of brands, products or companies and ask customers which they are familiar with. Companies with high brand awareness will likely be strategically focused on economies of scale.

PART 3: Competitive Analysis - Customer Captivity

Marketing A New Product - Customer captivity my second primary competitive advantage is called customer captivity. Customer captivity is somewhat like customer loyalty but it's not just that customers stay with you because they love your product or your brand. It's that there are structural reasons why they stay with you. There are structural reasons that make it difficult or expensive to leave you where competing products are. There are three sources of customer captivity. The first is search costs. These are the time, effort and resources required to go and find a replacement for your product.

A good example of a product with high search costs is one that has been customized. It is difficult to find a replacement for a customized product. Therefore customers tend to be more captive when solutions are customized to them. You can enhance search costs by adding customized features to your product run making the buying process feel as though the solution is customized. The second source of competitive advantage is switching costs. These are the costs incurred by customers in transitioning from one company to a competing company.

A good example of this is a product that requires a lot of training to use. If you have to learn a whole new system in order to use a competing product then you're going to be resistant to switching to a competitor. The third source of customer captivity is habit formation. Products that are used daily in purchases that happen virtually automatically build habit or inertia for example. People tend to be more loyal to Coca-Cola than to car brands because soda is bought more frequently than automobiles are. The role of a product marketing manager will vary from company to company but there are almost always going to be ways that can enhance customer captivity.

If you have a lot of influence over the product you can push for features that have daily use for customized or personalized dashboards. These will make customers resistant to switching in one. The long term profitability of the company. If you don't have a lot of control over the product itself. There are still ways to enhance customer captivity. For example you can push for long term contracts or for landing pages that make the customer feel as though she or he is getting a customized offer. Also as a strategic marketer you can choose to focus on those customers that are the most captive and then focus your acquisition efforts on them specifically.

PART 4 : Competitive Analysis - Marketing Strategy & Tactics

The third approach to competitive analysis is looking at marketing strategies and tactics. Let's start by analyzing strategy. The first part of strategy is looking at the target market. By this I don't just mean the target customer. I mean the entire target market, which is defined by the five C's. In other words, customers, competitors, collaborators, context and company. You can identify these in many different ways. Look at your competitor's ads and see who they are trying to target. Use websites like Similarweb to figure out what keywords they are using. Do a search for your competitors in the word partnership to identify who their collaborators are. Look at research reports or Google Trends to identify trends in the market.

All of these help you map out the target market of your competitors. The second part of strategy is the value proposition. This is how value gets created in the target market for three groups of people: customers, collaborators and the company. The value proposition isn't a single benefit. It is all the benefits, the various ways that value is created. For example, your competitor might help customers by making them do things faster and also cheaper. If this is true, then you have to wonder why customers would ever buy from you. Competitors also create value for collaborators by offering them special deals or perhaps giving them cash back for referrals.

None of this information is going to be laid out nicely in a report for you. So you have to dig into the competitor's websites and social media channels. You can also speak to their customers, your own customers, and look at news reports to piece the value proposition together. Once you understand what target market your competitor operates in and how it creates value in that market, you understand their marketing strategy. Next, you'll want to analyze the marketing tactics. These are popularly known as the Four P's. I don't actually use the four P's framework because it's not robust enough. I use the 70s or seven tactics. These are price communication, brand, product service, incentives and distribution.

Often when marketers create a strategic map, they'll use price as the primary basis of positioning. This may be helpful for you, but these days, price isn't always the most important differentiator. These days, vertical differentiation in which higher priced products are simply better is not very sophisticated. Consumers have different needs and value things differently. That's why brands and communication are important in understanding the competition.

SaaS Positioning Worksheet - Part A

This is a SaaS positioning worksheet, a spreadsheet that I put together for you. And what you're going to be able to do is start filling in notes on the right here for each of these different categories that I've listed and just just download the files, start filling it out. The way I want you to approach this is to think of it as a brainstorming exercise. So just kind of jot down what you know right now, refine it later as you get more information. You can leave holes in it. It's not meant to be this kind of linear step by step.

This is the way that you have to approach positioning, because with positioning there's going to be some jumping around. There's going to be some qualitative research that then you validate with quantitative research, and particularly if you're an early stage startup, you're going to do a lot of changes and you need to be agile when you're thinking about this kind of positioning exercise. So let's take a look at where we're going to begin, which is the product attributes. So this is essentially the supply side. It's what you're able to supply the target customers and I have here features, benefits, use cases, jobs to be done, outcomes, transformations, product categories, unique attributes.

So there's going to be some overlap here, right? Whether you call something a use case or a job to be done or transformation doesn't really matter. I'm just kind of using different terms here to get your creativity going to get you thinking about things that perhaps you hadn't thought of before. And sometimes it helps if you think of it as a job to be done instead of a use case, or if you think of it as perhaps a unique attribute instead of a point of difference feature. So just start writing notes here. If there is redundancy, if things are repeated in different categories, that's fine. So starting just kind of lists out the different features that you have.

Start listing out the different benefits and they don't necessarily need to be aligned to a specific feature. There could be whole clusters of features that produce some sort of benefit like save time, save money, etc., or speed up or automate. I want you to think about the specific use cases where people could potentially use your product and you may have some idea of what use case is most important. And then later, when we look at customers, we may find out, oh, you were actually wrong. It was actually a different use case that they valued more. Or what you may find out is they only valued one use case, even though you were trying to say that you were an all in one comprehensive solution. That's something I often see in SAS, where people think being all in one all encompassing is a value proposition. And then later when you actually research target customers, you realize that they don't, they don't really care about that.

They don't want it all in one solution. They just want that one key thing that you do really well, you put down the jobs to be done, the things that they want accomplished. So they're hiring your product to achieve something, to do a job like they would hire an employee. And you gotta think through what is that job that your product's doing? Think about outcomes and transformation. So often what you're really doing with sales marketing is you're selling a transformation, you're selling an outcome rather than necessarily selling a specific feature or something like that. In some cases, in a lot of cases, you also need to think about the categories that you're participating in. So there may be existing product categories you can go to CAP, Taraji to crowd, etc., see what those categories are.

And later when we start looking at competitors, you can start thinking about, well, maybe you can just own the category, right? If there aren't a lot of competitors and you're new and innovative, then the category may actually become your positioning. And lastly here, I have unique attributes. So these may be at the product level or could just be kind of your financial model, like maybe you're free or maybe you really you provide things on a usage basis instead of a monthly basis. Or it could really be fundamental differences in how your product works. Like maybe it uses artificial intelligence where other products don't. So once you looked at the supply side, now let's look at the demand side. What are customers actually demanding?

What are their needs? And I'm starting here with pain points because if you solve a pain point like a red hot pain, that's kind of the easiest thing to sell into the market. And those pains may vary by target. So, for example, Target A could be a specific industry or it could be a specific persona. So it might be the CEO target, could be the CFO, or it could be a completely different industry depending on how you segment and depending on whether you're doing a count based marketing. How you define targets may vary, and it also may mean the pain points, the priorities, etc. will vary based on those different people or there's different companies or consumers that you're targeting. So the first pain point I want to start with is what the customer has on top of mind every day. They have some sort of pain. Maybe they don't have enough sales, maybe they're just sick of doing something manually.

I don't know what is top of mind for them. And the important thing to recognize is that what's top of mind for them may be completely unrelated to your product. Do not assume that your product needs to solve a problem that's top of mind for them. It's often the case with SAS that you're actually trying to market something that is not top of mind for the buyer. It's something that may be top of mind at a particular time when a particular event happens, like a lawsuit or technical breakdown of their existing software or maybe when a virus hits or something like that. But generally day to day they may not be thinking about it. If they are, then that's great and that's going to be easier to market.

Now, the other type of pain points I want you to think about are specifically related to your category, your product, or your solutions. So maybe they're sick of other competing solutions that they use and that they don't provide this or they don't use artificial intelligence or their predictive analytics is wrong, or the automation is too slow or the automation is out of sync. There could be all sorts of pain points centered around what it is that you're selling. And there's also the flip side. So often with positioning, we're focused on the negative. What is the problem that we're solving? But we also need to think about the high level aspirations.

What do they want? What is it? What does the target customer really want? Do they want to be a $1,000,000,000 company? Is it an entrepreneur that just wants to retire with $1,000,000 in his or her bank account? I don't know what it might be. The other thing that you want to do is hone in on specific frustrations that the targets have with the status quo. And the status quo might be spreadsheets. It might be an employee that does a job that SAS could, it might be pen and paper, it could be just notes in a filing cabinet. I don't know what that might be next. Often it's good to have a list of the top priorities.

Like these are the main things that the target customers care about. And there may be five. There may be ten depending on how much data you have access to or how many people you've spoken to. And another thing here, and this becomes more relevant when you're getting deep into research and maybe you're working with a research company, is the willingness to pay. So the willingness to pay to solve pain point A may be different from pain point B, and the willingness to pay for specific features may be higher for some than for others. Another key thing to evaluate is the current text act.

So often the first question that somebody might have when they're considering your saz is does it work with what we use right now? So does it work with their ERP? Does it work at their CRM? Does it work with their practice management system? Does it work with our word processor, whatever that is? It's important to take a look at their text act to kind of lay that foundation of what you're going into. Because if you're a standalone product that doesn't integrate with what they're using, they may or may not want that. In some cases they may, because it's less complicated for them technically, but it's also going to be a pain in the bottle later in terms of saving time, etc..

Another thing to jot down here is the barriers they have to reaching their goals. So if we know their high level aspirations or just kind of their mid term goals, what are their barriers to getting there? And it's possible your SAS is removing those barriers to help them get to that goal more quickly. Now, something I want to point out when you're doing customer research is that typically you start with qualitative research and the most basic form of that is just asking on Korra, asking on Reddit groups, subreddits asking on Facebook, groups, asking on social media like your own personal network, perhaps on a LinkedIn post asking in Slack channels. That's probably the easiest way to start getting this kind of research. Then what I would move into is emails or perhaps WhatsApp messages or whatever where you're getting direct feedback from people.

Now, one of the hardest things is to actually get people on the phone to have a conversation. That's kind of the gold standard for qualitative research, is to actually spend half an hour on the phone to kind of get ideas, get insights from those target customers, the people that are in the target customer group you're going after. But it's very hard to do that. So one of the ways to convince somebody to actually show up for a phone call is to pay them, say, we're going to give you a $100 Amazon gift card, $50 Amazon gift card for input. You can do that with email, too. So one of the problems is if you just go broad and start saying, okay, anybody who volunteers, we're going to get feedback from them.

You may not necessarily get the CEO of a Fortune 500 company. You may not necessarily get the people you want, but if you're paying and you're incentivizing people to provide you insights, then you're more likely to get your actual target customers. Now qualitative is the most important because it's where you start and it's where you kind of lay the field of what needs to be considered. The second stage is quantitative. So this is when you typically do a survey. I'm going to talk later about different ways to quantify, but surveys are how you kind of figure out which of these things is most important and what is the relative importance to other aspects. And that's going to help you later determine what your positioning should actually be.

Now, something I want to point out is that there is a limitation to the information that you can get from customers because customers only know so much. And although they may think that your product's most important because it solves A or does B, they may not realize what you're capable of, they may not realize how you create value. So don't assume that your positioning needs to rely purely on what customers say. Sometimes it means figuring out what customers need or what their future needs will be, even if they don't realize it. So I put this as a separate category because I think it's just so important. But figuring out the level of awareness or education that the customer has and some people, they're not even aware that they have a problem, they don't know that this is an issue.

And that's where the majority of your customers may be, potential customers. They may also not even be aware of the category. So maybe you're a CRM, they don't know CRMs exist. Sometimes that's the case or they don't even know that term CRM. Then there are people that are just product unaware, so they don't they don't know about your specific brand, they don't know about your specific offering. But then there are people that are aware. So when you're a larger company, or perhaps you're in a super niche where everybody knows you, even though you're not a large company, then they're aware of your product. So the positioning will vary depending on the level of awareness that you figure out or you guess at where customers are in their kind of awareness funnel, if you will. So for example, positioning yourself as the best CRM.

Assumes that they know what the product category is, right? You're the best CRM, But if most people in your target customer group are not even aware that they have a problem and don't know, don't know the category, CRM positioning yourself as the best CRM is pointless. It's messaging that doesn't resonate. Now, let's say you're in a market where most people are already aware that your product exists. Then taking this, positioning this, trying to educate them on the product doesn't doesn't really make any sense. You've got to go deeper than that.

Now, the last thing I put here is objections to buying or trying, and that's something you need to address based on customer's awareness, because they're going to have a whole series of objections to why, oh, we don't need to use that category or we don't need to use your product, or we think that category is super expensive when actually it's not, or we think there's going to be an expensive licensing deal when actually it's just month to month sales or we think we don't have a problem. We've got to figure out and surface what those objections are because hammering and addressing each of those one by one can be one of the most guaranteed ways to actually get people to act, particularly when you're doing something like a long form, direct response, letter, email, etc.. So we've looked at the product supply, we've looked at the demand, we've looked at the level of customer awareness.

Now let's analyze the competition, because the positioning you take is going to depend on how crowded the space is with your competitors and the amount of value that you deliver is contextual and based on how much value the competing solutions have. So first thing I would do is put in the direct competitors, and these are going to be other people that basically provide the same software as you or very similar. But then there's also kind of perhaps indirect competitors. So this might be the status quo. So using spreadsheets or Excel, maybe what they're doing, they may be using pen and paper, they may be using an employee.

These aren't technically direct competitors, but they're solutions that compete with yours because people may object to using your software when they think, Oh, well, Ted can do that, or we have Excel to do that to do this, or we have Google Docs, which is free. Why do we need your surveying tool, whatever. So by analyzing the competition, then we're able to go back to our product and figure out what things are actually points of difference that make us different from our competitors, what are the points of parody? So the things that we actually have are very similar to our competitors, maybe we didn't realize it, maybe we thought we were special.

Turns out we're not really that special. It turns out a lot of the competitors offer what we do and we didn't know. And then there's points of irrelevance. So there are things that your competitors highlight and there are things that you highlight that are actually irrelevant. They're not things that customers actually care about. And in a lot of cases. Actually, the things that you think make you good are actually making you bad. So, for example, maybe you have a very advanced integration that carries tons of information from one system to the next, and you think, Wow, that's awesome. We're able to deliver everything or we're able to offer full customization. You customize everything, but the customer is thinking time, I want to save time.

Why do I want all this information going from system A to B if that just means the processing time is going to take longer? Why do I want to do all these customizations with my Android device when I just want it to be automated. I want it to speed up the process, not slow me down. So those are things that are actually value leaks. So to some extent there are points of irrelevance, but they're also points of negative value. All right. Now another thing that I want to address here is categorization. So you need to figure out if you are a business to business, non strategic purchase, a business to business, strategic purchase, a business to consumer purchase, or are you some sort of hybrid and you can jot whatever notes you want into the hybrid chapter.

SaaS Positioning Worksheet - Part B

So what is a business to business? Non strategic purchase versus a business to business? Strategic purchase. This is something I've talked about in my other Books. It's something I've written about and it's information that's based on the research of James Anderson, who is a business to business marketing professor from Kellogg. He's been featured in books by Harvard Business Review, talking about strategic marketing. You can see Harvard Business Review articles with him talking about this. And basically what a strategic purchase is, is when your product helps a company differentiate their product to their customers.

Now in cases like that. Differentiation matters a lot. How you are different from your competitors really, really matters because you are fundamentally changing how a company distinguishes itself from competitors in the market. And the example I usually cite here is Jungle Scout. Jungle Scout is software for Amazon sellers. It is a strategic purchase. The reason it's a strategic purchase is because Jungle Scout helps Amazon sellers determine what portfolio of products they need to sell to their customers. That is the fundamental variable that distinguishes one Amazon seller from another, the portfolio of products that they sell. But there are lots of things that Amazon sellers do and buy that have nothing to do with differentiating their product. So, for example, automating back end accounting, that is not a strategic thing. That is not how one Amazon's seller distinguishes themselves from.

Another problem I see with SaaS a lot of the time is people behave by default because they're oblivious to the fact that there is such a thing as a non strategic purchase and so many SAS or non strategic purchases, things that automate your back end office, things like plugins for your website. So many of these automated SAS offerings, plug-ins, integrations are non strategic. They're not helping companies differentiate themselves. So when you're trying to market something like that, your positioning shouldn't talk about really high level benefits.

Like we're going to explode your growth, we're going to revolutionize your business, we're going to make you so much more money and grow your profits. That is not correct positioning. You are not, you're not at that high level. You're a functional offering that does some operational optimization. Don't try to be something you're not. Now, the differentiation you're going to focus on is not fundamentally about your value proposition. It's going to be about things like do you have 24 hour support? Is your sales process easy? Can we have a money back guarantee? Is it easy to work with you? Is it easy to integrate? Is this going to be a pain in the butt for me as a director in a Fortune 500 company to buy your solution?

Because it's less likely to make me look bad. It's going to eat up less of my time. Those types of tactical operational sales process differentiators are what matter when you're selling a non strategic purchase. Now, with business to consumer positioning can look a lot different because in cases like this, things like emotion matter more. Uh, perhaps not as much as people tend to think, as I demonstrated when I showed the research from McKinsey. But there's certainly a bigger element of psychological value with a lot of consumer products and positioning can just move in a very different direction when you're not doing business to business.

And then there's hybrid models where basically you need to position yourself to, for example, the business to business buyers, but position yourself differently with the business to consumer, perhaps through sales enablement that you provide the businesses that are buying your product and then marketing it to consumers. All sorts of considerations with hybrid models. Now I have a category here that may be relevant for you, perhaps more relevant to companies that have been around for a long time. But repositioning now, often what you may do when you first start out before you have tons of funding, before you go public, whatever is, you take some sort of narrow position.

And then what we see with companies as they get bigger if you tend to take a broader positioning. So I just wrote some notes here about perhaps your long term plan. Maybe you have a ten year or 20 year plan for your business you're planning to commit to for a long time. Let's talk about what the positioning should be now and then how you kind of see that evolving over time. So, for example, with me, I'm right now positioned in this Book as a SaaS marketing expert, which I am. However, I'm also thinking long term that I really want to transform people's lives. I really want to help people not just with their SaaS businesses, not just with their marketing, but fundamentally with their life.

How do they become a better person? But right now, I'm not positioned in that space. I'm positioned as the sales marketing guru. But you can see that when you're thinking about long term horizons, your positioning can get much broader. Okay. So this loosely speaking, this is kind of like a step by step how you kind of hone in on your own positioning. So you start with product attributes, customer needs, and then you kind of gradually move down. And then ultimately you get to prioritization. And this is where you narrow in on a lot of cases. It might be one benefit, one use case, one job to be done, or it might be a product category.

Your positioning could be maybe three benefits, two benefits, a feature and a benefit or just one feature if that feature is unique and provides a lot of value. So how you prioritize is one of the one of the difficult strategic decisions you can make. And there are different ways to do it. The gold standard is, is some sort of quantification model where you've brainstormed all kinds of positioning directions at the top, but then you quantify it to hone in on exactly what the positioning should be. But positioning is not just a science, it's also an art. So sometimes your positioning is just an intuitive thing. It's not necessarily a scientific quantitative process. So one way is to start with just what is logical positioning.

You've done this brainstorming, you've done this analysis. What seems like the best fit. Another thing to do is to actually quantify each attribute that you have. Usually , each benefit adds a financial value to it. So you automate this, you streamline that, you blah, blah, blah. Well, it may turn out that the automation of A and B saves companies $10 Million a year. And the other things that you do are barely making a dent in their finances. So your positioning is probably going to be around that around the $10 Million that you save because you do this streamlining or something like that. Sometimes it's hard to do, particularly in a startup. Now if you're a mid sized company, it's going to be pretty easy because you have a lot of case studies. You have credibility with customers. You can do case study analysis to kind of figure out how much value was created from each of the benefits you deliver. And then you can hone the positioning around the strongest financial benefit.

Now you can also quantify your attributes in non financial ways. So things like how much time did this save? For example, if feature A saves you 10 hours a week, feature B saves you 20 hours a week, then positioning around feature B probably makes more sense or taking the positioning around time savings in general and then just using the various features and how much time they save is a reason to believe the to believe in the positioning. Another way to quantify and prioritize, to kind of hone in on your positioning is survey results. So you can go to a website like sentiment. So what sentiment is, is just a website for getting panel data. So for example, you could survey marketing directors and you can just type in a quote, request to say, okay, I want 50 responses from VP of marketing companies with 200 plus employees in the USA and they'll give you a quote. So you might pay, I don't know, $1,000 to survey these people in your target customer group.

And then you ask them ten questions about the above to kind of figure out, okay, what actually matters the most to them? What are their biggest pain points? ET cetera. And that can help you make a decision for your positioning. Now, if you're not that sophisticated or you don't have that much time or you're just too agile and you're not sure you could rely on interview results. So just use qualitative data to make a decision on your positioning. You could use focus groups. So I've done positioning research with focus groups. So for example, I did in San Diego and then I also did in Chicago and then kind of compare the two.

We had different segments. So there were like three major segments that we had focus groups for to get the creative juices going among people that were in those given segments. And that helped us give an idea not just about the positioning but also honing in on the target customer as well. So you can couple positioning research with marketing research when you're doing market strategy research when you're doing focus groups. Because it can be pretty expensive and time consuming. You may want to kind of bundle, bundle various research together there. Now, one of the other things to do is you may have different positioning directions.

You want to go with a new product or a new feature or maybe a new mobile app version of your desktop product, something like that. One way to determine the positioning is just figure out which one makes the most sense based on the wider company strategy. So that's more of an intuitive or kind of non non survey, non research based way to determine the positioning. The other thing is just to make a very educated assumption about which attribute creates the most value for the potential buyer, and if it creates the most value, it's probably going to be the best positioning for you. Now, the last way that I have here to prioritize, figure out what your positioning is ultimately is empirical test results so you can do things like A, B tests with your email through something like Lem List or MailChimp.

If you're you're targeting existing people in your database, you can do empirical tests with Google ads, with LinkedIn ads, with Facebook ads, You could do tests through surveys, you could do tests through behaviors, you could do field tests where you're actually putting different positioning, packaging into the market, into stores and see which ones people buy. You could do it in digital marketplaces, like maybe run, you know, it's not going to be an exact AB test because app marketplaces aren't going to let you do that. But you could say, okay, we're going to run this one for a week, another one for a week. And assuming there's no huge difference between those weeks, you can say, Oh, well, we got much more results from the app listing that focused on X than we did with Y. So that would be an empirical way to determine your positioning.

Brand Marketing Introduction

He paid just $35 for its logo. Today, Interbrand ranks it the 10th most valuable brand in the world at $50 billion. The lesson here is that the number one driver of a brand's value is not its design, it's how well known it is. And there's a simple formula to make your brand well known. Or, in other words, a formula to make your brand valuable. And that formula is reach plus frequency plus memorability. That is your formula for brand success. If you don't reach a lot of people, you cannot make a lot of sales. Reach is the ceiling on how valuable your brand can be. There are some easy ways to increase your reach.

For example, video ads on YouTube are one of my favorites. That's because YouTube counts a view typically as around 30s, which means people actually watched it and they might remember your brand. You can also run video ads on places like Facebook and LinkedIn. You can do billboards and other out-of-home advertising, which I've done before. This work for companies like Brex as well as established large businesses, you can find influencers on places like Sparktoro or Twitch. You can also create interesting stories around your brand to get published in major news outlets. Number two frequency. People might hear about your brand once. They might hear about it twice. In fact, they might even buy your brand and still forget about you.

You need to market your brand continuously throughout the year to stay top of mind. The idea here is that people will think of your brand when a need arises and then they buy from you.

So you need to constantly remind them that you exist. Easy ways to increase frequency include automated emails with tools like MailChimp and Lemlist or retargeting ads with tools like Facebook. Number three Memorability research has shown that people typically cannot identify which brand paid for a particular ad. Often this is because most brands in a product category look exactly the same. Take, for example, roofers.

A lot of their logos are probably pictures of houses. You can't remember any particular roofing company because they all look the same. So the key to memorability is really just looking and sounding different. Take, for example, the insurance company Lemonade. It doesn't make any sense that an insurance company is named Lemonade or that they use a pink color. But that's the point. It's memorable. It's odd it stands out. Research also shows that the easiest way to be memorable with your branding is with some sort of mascot, so you can try to be memorable with a different logo, a different name, different font, etcetera. But the number one driver is really a mascot or something similar to a mascot such as a spokesperson or maybe a large object. So think of Tony the Tiger, or in business to business, think of Salesforce with its cute little animals.

You might hear a lot about brand, personality, brand, purpose and brand love. I heard a lot about these because in my career over ten years ago, I was working with these types of concepts and branding small businesses. So what you need to focus on are reach, frequency and memorability. The other thing to keep in mind throughout this Book is that brands are not the same thing as products. These are separate marketing assets that create value in different ways.

Often the product creates value in a way that is very tangible, whereas brands typically create value in more psychological ways. I was a global brand manager for Sony PlayStation. I studied brand management at the number one marketing school in the US. Philip Kotler's Kellogg School of Management.

Notes from Byron Sharp

Let's take some more time to go through some key notes from Byron Sharp's research. One of the reasons that I'm spending so much time on this is because the conclusions are not intuitive. If you rely on your intuition, you're highly likely to make poor product marketing decisions. So once again, you should prioritize acquisition over loyalty. This grossly simplifies the role of marketing in that fundamentally, you're going to be gauged on how well you're able to acquire new customers. This means emphasizing things like customer marketing. So for example, sending emails to existing customers or focusing on loyalty programs, focusing on customer success enablement. These things should be moved to the bottom of your priority list focused on new customer acquisition. That's fundamentally what drives growth.

Now, two of the most important concepts that Byron Sharp tells us is that fundamentally what you're trying to do in the marketing world is build mental availability and physical availability. So mental availability basically means mind space. Are you in people's minds? Do they think of you in particular? Do they think of you in specific contexts or what he calls category entry points or what you might call a buying situation? Or when I look at McKenzie's research, you might call it like a trigger. So for example, if you're hungry at breakfast, do you think of Starbucks? Do you think of McDonald's? What comes immediately to mind?

In business to business, you just had a security threat to your computer systems. Who do you think of what brand comes to mind? So mental availability is really what you're focused on here. It's a more sophisticated understanding of basically brand awareness. Now physical availability is things like are you available on the shelf? If you're selling a physical product, if you're selling a digital product or you're focusing on digital distribution, then you're going to be thinking about are you showing up? When people search on Google, are you showing up when they search on Amazon?

Are you easy to find essentially what physical availability is? So a lot of the time what marketers are really focused on is things like Google search engine ads, which are basically increasing your physical availability. But when we're talking about advertising, usually what we're talking about is mental availability, increasing the probability that people think of you in certain buying contexts. So that's a huge part of the advertising world that a lot of digital marketers in particular myths and something that product marketers definitely need to be more focused on that kind of wide reach awareness marketing to build mental availability and that that takes a lot longer to realize the results from compared to something like physical availability, but it can really drive growth.

So what we learn here is that brands or products fundamentally compete in these two spaces in terms of mental space and physical space. And that's basically how you're competing with other products for market share. And those that are losing mental availability will ultimately start to lose market share. And one of the key things here with mental availability is tying your product to as many category entry points as is feasible given your marketing budget. So you want to associate your brand with multiple situations, multiple jobs to be done, multiple trigger events, etc..

Now, the other thing here is that distinctive brand assets matter. So fundamentally, when you're thinking about your product and how it gets branded, you need to think about distinctiveness. Too many product marketers are just going to do what their competitors are doing. They're going to use the same colors, the same imagery. One of the reasons they do this is because certain imagery has logical meaning to it. So, for example, something like an octopus, which would suggest multiple connections. So if you're an integrator, you're likely to use an octopus.

Your competitor might use an octopus. If you're dealing with global security threats, you might use a globe as your symbol, but so would your competitors. So what Byron Sharp advises is that you pick things that are essentially meaningless. So something like a peacock or a gecko and just make it only will make it distinctive so that people are able to distinguish your brand from others. Because the last thing is the last thing that you want to do is advertise something that actually benefits your competitor. So if your competitor is associated with a globe and you use a globe in your imagery, then you're basically going to help them in their market share.

Another non-intuitive conclusion from the research is that you need to pursue light or infrequent buyers. So even with large companies like Coca Cola, what we see is that half their customer base may only buy their product once or twice a year, and that's really surprising. But that's really the key to growth, is how do you get those people that are very infrequent even considering you or your competitors? And the way that you do that is by running continuous advertising campaigns so that you're able to have some integration into people's memories so that they're more likely to buy from you. So target the light buyers, target all category buyers, including your existing customers. But don't, don't focus on your existing customers.

And the other thing that you can consider is people who will become category buyers. So people that are soon to enter the category. And in business to business, this may be a case where perhaps the only people that consider buying your products are VP's, but in the future, the directors of today are going to become the VP tomorrow. So you might choose to target the directors as well, using something like LinkedIn ads as an example. Another thing is that the efficiency of targeting isn't as important as the reach. So this is a fundamental error marketers make is that they're very focused on spear phishing activities where the targeting is as precise as possible so that there's zero wastage. But the bigger picture, distinguishing the forest from the trees, is how many people you're reaching.

And if you can get a ton of more reach, even if some of the people you reach are irrelevant, it's still worth it. The other thing I would keep in mind for my experience is that reach is not that expensive. You would be amazed at what $100 in Facebook ads per month will get you in terms of reach. And I'm reaching millions of people with my advertising right now. Advertising should be continuous. So we talked about the importance of reach. But the other factor here is recency. Are you thinking about the time when somebody is ready to buy something and it's very hard to predict when people are going to be in that situation despite a lot of efforts to try to predict that. So the best practice is basically to run your advertising continuously.

Don't do pulsing or flighting unless you're highly seasonal or you have a strong justification for why so continuous advertising increases the likelihood somebody will consider your brand, your product. Now there is a lot of misunderstanding about how advertising works. I saw on LinkedIn recently someone who decided to stop all of their Facebook ads, I believe it was, and they noticed that, oh, revenue didn't go down. And if you ask people, does advertising work on you? They'll say no. And a lot of these are actually misunderstandings of how advertising works. So basically, advertising is a weak force and what it does is it just nudges you. It just slightly increases the probability that someone will buy from you by your brand. But even though that impact is very weak when you scale it over all buyers in the category essentially over time, so you're continuously advertising for maximum reach.

The impact is actually huge. So even though the impact on the probability is quite small, you scale it over a million people, 100,000 people. That impact is large. So what there isn't necessarily the impact of I just turn on advertising. So sales immediately went up or I just shut off advertising and sales immediately went down. That's not how advertising works. It's a long term thing that increases the probability over time, but that impact is huge and it's essential to growth. Now, when you're talking about direct response advertising, sure, you can see your sales immediately go up, but you're really not focused on long term growth in that case, and the impact is very minimal in the long term.

The primary function of branding really goes back to its original purpose. So you think of branding as actually taking that hot item and branding something, you're basically just telling the buyer who made the product, and that's fundamentally what branding is. People get caught up in the meaning of branding, which in some contexts is important in my opinion. But with Byron Sharp, he's really just talking about associating your brand assets with essentially the brand name. Another thing is that there's this kind of highfalutin attitude in marketing that we're trying to create evangelists. We're trying to make people fall in love with our brand. But the reality is that buyers rarely think of brands. They're not obsessing over you. They're worried about their movies. They're worried about their kids.

They're worried about getting soccer practice. So the big problem is not really what they think about you because they don't really care that much. The biggest challenge is just getting them to think of you at all. So what they think of you or generally speaking, positioning is not as important as just getting them to think about you. And that's by doing things like broad, rich advertising. You don't want to give people a reason not to buy. So there's going to be tons of barriers to purchase. So this might be that the bundle is too big. The pricing options don't cater to your needs. So often what you need to do is actually just mimic your competitors and provide exactly the variance, the portfolio of options that they offer as well.

Now their conclusion is that mass advertising works, even though targeting has become sort of the default assumption in the marketing world. I know from experience that mass marketing does work. I run very large TV advertising and I've seen sales spike as a result. Loyalty programs generally don't work, and the reason is that loyalty is largely out of our control. People will stop buying products for reasons that have very little to do with what the seller is controlling. Loyalty tends to be higher for larger brands. So there's this myth. Generally speaking, in the marketing world, we can create niche brands that really make people fall in love with us. And that's how we're going to grow. But that's not really true. It's actually the larger brands that have larger loyalty. And one of the reasons is that loyalty is less a function of love and more a function of convenience or lock-in capabilities.

Focusing on high volume buyers specifically isn't generally a good strategy. One of the reasons is that heavy buyers become light buyers in the future and vice versa. So it's best to simply have a wider reach and reach all category buyers. Another key thing is that reach is more important than frequency. This is a problem that I frequently run into when I'm running ads such as video ads on LinkedIn or on Facebook is that the frequency tends to get very high. Now there's an optimal frequency, perhaps around two or three per week, but in some cases you may want to get your frequency down to just for the entire campaign, slightly over one. The biggest factor here is increasing the reach because there's diminishing returns from exposing somebody to your ad multiple times.

Now, one thing you need to do is when you're in a tool like Facebook ads, you need to go to the column chapter and select delivery, and then you're able to see the reach and the frequency, make sure that frequency is not getting too high if it is what you need. What you need to do is add capping, frequency capping if you're able to, or perhaps even lowering the budget or increasing the targeting so you're able to reach more people. Differentiation and error positioning are overrated. Instead, what you need to focus on is superficial distinctiveness through things like your brand assets. And one of the reasons is that this is a problem. Focusing too much in differentiation forces you into a niche market or appealing to a small group of people. And that's not how you drive growth.

You drive growth by appealing to many people in many different buying situations. Price cuts are generally a bad idea, except in situations where it's designed to maintain relationships with retailers or partners. So sometimes you have to do price cuts to be able to get special displays, for example, in supermarkets. The profile of your customers should map the profile of category buyers. So this is really interesting because if you look at data on who your customers are or you might notice that, hey, they're somewhat unique, maybe they're more likely to be women or they're more likely to be entrepreneurs, or they're more likely to be X, Y and Z. But this is not actually a cause for celebration.

It's actually a symptom that you're not appealing to enough people. And that's really going to hinder your growth. It's going to hinder your market share. You're not going to be able to achieve economies of scale. And therefore, you're likely not to have sustained profitability as your competitors. So what you want to do is look at all category buyers and get some data on that, see what they look like, what the segmentation is. And generally speaking, that's who your profile should be. And the last thing I want to point out here is that not only are you competing with competitors for physical availability and mental availability, but you're also in a continuous battle against memory decay. So people are going to forget about you. They're not going to think of you at all. So this is one of the reasons that you have to have continuous effort with your advertising so that people are able to think of you, particularly when the need arises, to to buy in your category.

1-Page Competitive Analysis Template Walk-through

This is a competitor analysis template that I developed after ten years in product marketing and teaching college level marketing. The big challenge with doing a competitor analysis is that it can be very overwhelming. There are dozens of competitors that you could be looking at and thousands of different tactics that you can evaluate. And those tactics are constantly changing with things like the website, which is frequently updated. So there's really no end to it. What I've done here is created a one page simple template that helps you focus on the things that really matter.

And one of the first things that really matters is competitive advantages. What these are is the elements that make it difficult to steal customers from your competitors or for you to take customers and market share away from your competitors. And there are really only four types of sustainable competitive advantage. The first is the switching and search costs. So in some cases it's actually expensive to switch from one provider of a product to another. An example of this is when you have software that's been custom tailored to you, you're basically stuck to the person that created the custom software because they understand it, they know how to maintain it, they know how to update it.

Whereas if you hire somebody new, that person needs to spend a lot of time and a lot of your money learning that custom software. So that's a key competitive advantage. The other is search costs. So these are things that make it difficult to find replacements for the product that you're currently using. An example of this would be if you are buying something that's highly specialized, like a certain IT specialist or a specialized professional, sometimes it's very difficult to find them, particularly in a specific region. Next is habituation. So for example, with Adobe Creative Suite, a lot of graphic designers are in the habit of using certain keyboard shortcuts, so their muscle memory keeps them stuck to that software because if they do switch to different software, they have to relearn all these habits.

Other examples would be products that are somewhat addictive, so things like Coca Cola would be an example. Arguably, the strongest competitive advantage that you can have is economies of scale. The best example of this would be something like a natural monopoly or duopoly. So if you're participating in a market that can really only support 1 or 2 providers of a product at scale, then if somebody tries to enter that market, they can't really do it because they can't match your price structure and the cost structure that goes along with it. So if competitors are able to sell products at a cheaper price and be more profitable than you, then it's going to be very, very difficult for you to steal customers away from them.

The last key competitive advantage is government protection. So these are things like patents and licenses that effectively make it illegal for competitors to take customers away from you or vice versa. So when I'm looking at competitor analysis, the first thing I like to look at is to make lists of do they have some sort of moat of competitive advantage that's built around them and based on these four things. So after looking at that, structurally, I get into the marketing strategy. And the first thing that you want to analyze is what target customers are your competitors going after. They may have a similar product to you. They may have similar services to you. But if they aren't actually going after the same customers, then they're not really your competitors. They may look like competitors, but your customers aren't going to see them as competitors, and neither will your competitors, even if they're using similar technology. The other thing, and I think this is probably the big thing with marketing strategy that product marketers miss is partners.

A huge part of your marketing strategy is who you partner with. So, for example, it might be your retailer, Walmart or Amazon. It might be certain marketplaces that you're participating in. It may be key influencers that are endorsing your product. This is very important because if your competitors are getting a lot of traction with large partners and you're not, then you're going to be left behind and you can actually replicate those exact partnerships, assuming that they're not exclusive. And if the partnerships are exclusive, then you can simply find a similar company to have an exclusive contract with. The other key part of the marketing strategy is the value proposition. So in what way are your competitors creating value in the market, particularly for customers, but also for partners? So for example, is it that they save time? Is it that they save money?

Is it that they fix some critical integration issue in that particular product? It might be very, very narrow, particularly if you're in a small market with small players or the value proposition may be very large, particularly when you're selling something like a suite of software solutions for small business and your competitors have a lot of venture capital to support them. Closely tied to the value proposition is the positioning. So usually this is one, maybe two features or benefits that your competitors are choosing to emphasize in their messaging to secure a certain place in the minds of the target customers. So somebody might position themselves around speed. They might position themselves around cost savings. So it's very important to understand how your competitors are positioning themselves.

And the easiest way to do that is to look at their home page. Their home page may have a tagline on it, and usually that gives you a sense of what kind of positioning they want in the minds of the customers. After doing the market strategy analysis. I like to look at the reviews because the reviews tell you if what your competitors are saying actually matches what they're delivering and the customer feedback is going to give you that. The first thing I like to do is look at a review source such as Google, for example. You can look at Facebook or G2 crowd. There are a number of different review resources that you should be looking at.

First thing I look at is just the numeric score. Is it a nine out of ten, four out of five, three out of five? But it's also very important to look at the notes because the notes give you the qualitative feedback that tell you whether the positioning is actually working. So if a company says that their product is very easy to use, but a lot of the notes that you're seeing in the reviews is that they're not easy to use. Then that means that the positioning is not really held superficially. They're making a promise, but ineffectively, they're failing to deliver on that promise. So that may mean that you have an open position in the market for you to fill by providing a superior product. After looking at the reviews, I like to look at the tactics and there are basically seven types of marketing tactics.

I use this because it's a more modern version of the four PS model that you're probably familiar with. First thing is that pricing is very important to understand pricing because it dictates supply and demand. If the price is very low, then what that probably means is your competitor has the size and the economies of scale to be able to deliver at a lower price. That may not be the case. And if it's not the case, then it probably means that they're not profitable. The packaging is also important, so it's not just what the price is, but also how they're clustering their prices into things like three different types of plants. How are they basing the pricing? Is it based on usage? Is it based on the number of users? There are a number of different variables that can drive pricing and making little tweaks to your pricing can actually have substantial effects on the demand for what you're selling.

Another thing is the brand. Brands play a more important role in some markets than others, so don't spend a lot of time on it if it doesn't really matter in your industry. The services are also important. So even if what you're marketing is not fundamentally a service, it may be that things like customer support or warranties play a substantial role in convincing people to buy the product. And then you want to look at the product features themselves, buy your competitor's product, do their free trial, get their samples, look at it, see if it actually does what they say it will do. Communication. This is one of the biggest parts of marketing.

It's usually where people start. So this is looking at things like the advertising, the social media posts, the website, the landing pages. It gives you a sense of how effective your competitors are at communicating to the target customers. Incentives and promotions can matter a lot. So things like coupons, time sensitive offers. And also you really want to consider the distribution or channels that your competitors are going through. So typically, a lot of time is spent looking at competitors' websites, but the website doesn't tell the whole picture. It could be that most of their sales are coming from Amazon or they're coming from Salesforce App Exchange or they're coming from apps.com.

So don't assume that the website is the most up to date version of how the competitor is marketing themselves. So after looking at the strategy, looking at the tactics, looking at the reviews, looking at the competitive advantages, there are a few key things that I really like to focus on in the end. First is the direct response offer. So are your competitors selling something like a demo or a free trial, or are they really pushing a coupon redemption? Because these little offers and how the messaging centers around the offers can make a huge difference in your conversion rate, your sales pipeline, and ultimately your sales.

Can also look at web traffic and authority. You can use things like Moz Semrush Spyfu to get a sense of how much share of voice your competitors have and how much you have compared to them. Keyword Rankings are also very important if you want to own a position in the market centered around certain keywords. Funding is important. You can use websites like Crunchbase to find out how much funding your competitors have. If they do have a lot of funding, then that means that they can probably have a broad value proposition or go after a broad market. If you have little funding, then you probably need to niche down, maybe focus on specific features and have your value proposition narrowed to go after perhaps a smaller industry like one industry or one specific type of customer because people with a lot of funding can afford to go broader. People with little funding can't do that, at least not yet.

Another thing that gives you a sense of size isn't just the funding, but also the number of employees. And I find that LinkedIn is one of the most reliable up to date ways to get this. And the last thing I'd like to do is just have general notes. So these could be notes of things that you noticed while you were analyzing the other aspects of your competitors. It could be looking at the notes in Salesforce. It could be talking to salespeople to see what they're saying about customers. And it could be from talking to customers themselves, looking not only at their reviews, but actually interviewing them and discussing with them. So this is an overview of my one page competitor template. It's available for free. Please click the link in the description and I'll send it to you right away.

Very Important Notes on Competitive Advantage

MOST companies do NOT have sustainable competitive advantages. They compete on efficiency. This is great news because it means new entrants (startup founders) can compete on a somewhat level playing field! Startups largely succeed by focusing on operating efficiently because they rarely benefit from significant barriers to entry, except in some cases such as when they have meaningful patents.

Efficient operation at a small scale requires focusing on a narrow product space or geography. 3 types of customer captivity: habituation, switching costs & search costs The best companies often benefit from economies of scale and some degree of customer captivity, even if that captivity is weak. Reference: Dr. Bruce Greenwald of Columbia Business School

7 Big Product Marketing Mistakes

Choosing your target customer is the most important strategic marketing decision. Strategy, however, is just a chosen pathway towards reaching a goal. Without first setting a goal, your targeting decisions are aimless. Many marketing managers assume that the ideal customer is the one who derives the most value from a product.

It is more accurate to say that the ideal customer is the one that is most likely to help you reach your goal. When I worked for Sony, I was charged with choosing the target customer for a new, highly innovative product. I thought I had found the perfect target as the product delivered on everything this segment wanted. The product-customer fit was perfect. There was just one colossal problem: that segment was incredibly small.

Even if most of that segment bought the product, they would barely have made a dent in Sony's financials. I had to pursue a larger segment — not because it aligned most with the value proposition — but because it was the only realistic path towards reaching the financial goal. When you make strategic decisions, distinguish the forest from the trees by remaining focused on your end goal. Usually this goal is a specific financial target with a time constraint. For example, the goal of generating $X million in one quarter constraints who you must target and what tactics you must employ to reach that audience quickly.

#2 not estimating demand early enough

I know companies that spent years developing products that flopped completely when they went to market. Only then do they discover that there was never really much demand for what they were building. This problem is very common with software products that mimic what's already on the market. This problem is also common with unique products that have little competition but also little demand.

Amazon sellers, for example, often sell creative products that generate no search volume. This "white space" or "blue ocean" strategy only works if you supply a market that has adequate demand. There are four key ways to avoid this problem: 1. Study products that are already selling well and improve on their deficiencies. Look at product reviews to see what new positioning your product can take. This approach is popular among ecommerce sellers.

It is also very common in publishing where "comps," comparable products, form the basis of sales forecasting. 2. Estimate demand using keyword research tools and sales-estimate tools such as Google Keyword Planner and Jungle Scout. 3. Borrow total addressable market (TAM) data from investor relations presentations for leading companies in your industry. 4. Conduct your own primary research, such as surveying a sample of prospective buyers to estimate demand.

#3 not giving partners strategic importance

Most product marketing managers equate "target market" to the target customer. But the target market includes more than just customers, it also includes target partners. Choosing the right partners is more important than choosing the right marketing tactics. A single contract with a large partner, for example, could generate more leads than ten years' worth of demand generation.

The challenge with partner marketing is that results are delayed. Partner programs and affiliate networks take time to build with tangible results realized in months rather than weeks. It is essential to get buy-in from the rest of your company as the ROI will not be immediate but will most certainly be significant.

#4 not quantifying your value proposition

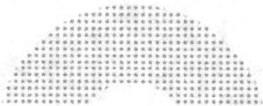

It's not always possible to quantify your value proposition, especially when your product's value is mostly psychological rather than financial. In many cases, however, the value you create can be measured quite precisely: each benefit can be quantified. For example, you might sell light bulbs that generate $X in energy savings, $Y in labor savings, and $Z in maintenance savings. If 90% of the value comes from energy savings then avoid positioning your product around labor and maintenance.

Assessments like these may make you realize that your positioning decisions were wrong all along. You weren't emphasizing the benefits that mattered most. Moreover, you may even discover that some of your "benefits" were actually destroying value.

#5 assuming
benefits are
more important
than features

Common marketing wisdom will have you believe that you should focus on benefits rather than features. This isn't universally true. Customers are often seeking specific features to solve immediate pains. Mapping out the customer journey will help you avoid this common mistake. Pay particular attention to "triggers," the events that motivate people to start seeking a solution. That trigger, for example, might be a feature deficiency in a competing product.

You cannot assume that the higher you move up in the value ladder the better your messaging will be. If this were true, all B2B marketing would center around the message of "make more profit," which doesn't communicate anything of value. Quite often features should take center stage, particularly when addressing technical audiences who balk at sales speak.

#6 using formal copywriting

Formal, grammatically correct language is great if you need the respect of academics, but the best copywriting is conversational. Most of the leading copywriters including John Caples and Bob Bly advocate a casual, conversational tone of voice. You should speak directly to your audience as though you were speaking to them face-to-face.

Colloquialisms, cheesy lines such as "but wait, there's more!" and gimmicks such as the ellipsis are all effective tactics. Demand generation legend Howard Sewell defends these tactics in his article "But Wait, There's More! Why Cheesy Copy Still Works."

#7 testing inconsequential tactics

Marketers have a peculiar fixation with testing tactics that generate very little lift. One common example is email timing. Managers agonize over whether an email should be sent Thursday afternoon or Saturday morning. Sometimes timing is crucial, such as when you release a movie and spend 90% of your budget over a two-week period. In most cases, however, email timing just does not matter.

What was true of direct mail in the 1980s is true of email today: you should test (a) the list (b) the offer and © the creative. Excessive optimization also occurs with websites and landing pages. A popular ethos today is that you should "test everything." In reality, whether your CTA is purple or green will make no material difference. Tweaking your website for minor conversion increases may be distracting you from other decisions that could double or quadruple your customer base.

Product differentiation and positioning are easily copied

Product differentiation and positioning are easily copied Product differentiation & positioning are easily copied... Consider LG capitalizing on Samsung's success with lifestyle televisions like the Serif and Frame. LG's "Pose" is a better product with nearly identical positioning.

Key lessons: 1. Differentiation & positioning are not sustainable competitive advantages because competitors can copy you. The most enduring competitive advantages are economies of scale & customer captivity. 2. Brands create value separately from products. People will prefer Samsung even when LG offers a better product with better technology. 3. Corporate brands (Samsung) are different from product-level brands (The Serif). 4. Brand marketing is essential.

History of Product Marketing

Typically product marketers will report to a director of marketing, a head of marketing or someone else in the marketing department. Occasionally, the product marketing manager is going to report directly to the CEO. But often what people are surprised by is when a product marketing manager reports to the head of product reports into the product team. This might come as a surprise. But if we look at the history of product marketing, it shouldn't be surprising at all because traditionally the role that product marketing managers played was actually performed by product managers.

So product managers would typically manage product development in the very early stages, and then they would also manage the products when those products went to market. So in the very late stages of the product life cycle. But in the 90s, what happened was this role split off from product management and became product marketing management. So that's the reason why a lot of the terminology is vestiges from this era. So, for example, product marketing managers often don't come up with a marketing plan.

They come up with a go to market plan because this is the terminology that was used in the product management days. But effectively when you come up with a comprehensive marketing plan, that is what a lot of people refer to as a go to market plan or sometimes mislabeled a go to market strategy. So this helps you understand the context for what product marketing really is. It is going to market products. It is also a more strategic component to traditional marketing. And the reason is because it's more closely tied to product management, which has a more strategic role rather than marketing communications, which is traditionally what marketers owned.

So the kinds of work that would. Or could be outsourced to an agency. That's what I would consider more traditional marketing. So it's like media buying, advertising, communications, that sort of stuff. Whereas the things that are a little bit closer to product management, that are a bit more strategic and things that are much more difficult to outsource, that's product marketing. So these are things like looking at the total addressable market, looking at analytics for the product itself and being more intimately tied to what's happening within the company and perhaps a little less externally focused on the kinds of things that an agency could manage.

Why PMMs Need to Understand

So I just explained what product marketing fundamentally is and why it is different from traditional marketing. Traditional marketing being more focused on marketing, communications and the kind of work that an external agency can do. But in this Book, I'm also going to go into great detail on demand generation, in great detail on other aspects of marketing communications.

Why am I doing that? I'm doing that because the role of product marketing management will vary depending on the size of the company and how mature their product marketing management team is. So often startups, let's say a series A, a pre-seed or a bootstrap startup will put out a job solicitation for a position called product marketers. Really, what these jobs are is not product marketing. It is marketing for products and when you're an early stage company, let's say you have less than 5 million, less than $10 million in revenue.

The primary function of marketing is basically demand generation, especially in the B2B space. Because these companies cannot have too long a focus and cannot be too strategically focused because they're too immature. They're not developed enough, and they need to be focused on generating revenue. And that's why you, as the product marketing manager, at least in title, have to take full control of the marketing plan and make sure that you're focused on demand generation. Otherwise, the company may not be around tomorrow because you haven't generated enough pipeline revenue for the sales team.

Now the sweet spot for product marketing management is mid sized companies. So this is maybe after $10 million in revenue, up to say $100 million in revenue. The reason is because at this point, it's not just about survival. It's not just about short term revenue and demand generation. This is when the core of what product marketing is becomes more important, and that is things like strategically defining what the target customer group is defining and laying out who the potential partners are, quantifying and identifying the value proposition and how to position yourself in the market.

Developing a more sophisticated approach to product launches. This kind of stuff is really established in mid-sized companies now at late stage companies, very large companies or companies that have tons of funding. What ends up happening is the role of product marketing starts to get split up. So a lot of that strategic research ends up going to customer insights teams, so people that are more focused on research or potentially external agencies that are commissioned to do market research. A lot of the tactical execution is delegated to other marketing teams, and the focus of product marketing becomes a little more focused on project management and pulling everything together.

So I would say that the core of product marketing starts to get established in those mid-sized companies, whereas when you're at smaller companies, you do need to be more focused on demand generation and marketing communications, which is part of the reason I'm going into so much detail on that in this Book. And I would say that because product management is so popular with tech companies that a lot of this has perhaps less to do with how mature the company is, but perhaps more on how much funding they have.

So a lot of these SaaS companies, for example, might get tons of funding even if they haven't been around for a while. In those cases, basically you're treating it as though it is a mid-sized company because of the amount of funding that's available. So that role of product marketing is going to vary depending on the size of the company, the extent to which they have funding and the extent to which they understand what product marketing is as a function as opposed to simply marketing products.

Managing Cannibalization

Cannibalization. Cannibalization is when you promote one product and hurt another. As a product marketing manager, you have to make difficult decisions that involve cannibalization. Should you take Google AdWords budget away from one product in order to promote a new product? Should you promote one type of conversion over another one? These are difficult decisions to make, so some analysis is helpful. One thing to consider is that size matters. Let's say, for example, that you have a very profitable product that generates $40,000 per year and you have another product that isn't quite as profitable but generates $5 million in revenue per year.

You might think it makes sense to promote the more profitable product, but in this case, size probably matters a lot more than profitability. A $40,000 product just isn't big enough to have an impact on your business. It may even be worth it just to drop the $40,000 product altogether from your product portfolio. That's because every product requires some level of fixed cost to support it, such as management resources. So in a case like this, you probably do not want to promote the smaller product if it means cannibalizing the larger product. But there are cases where the reverse may be true.

For example, if you forecast high growth of the small market for the next five years and a decline in the larger market, it's probably a good idea then to cannibalize the larger product with the smaller one. So from a marketing perspective, that would mean taking up valuable real estate on your website and your advertisements and in your marketing budget with promotions of the new product. There are also situations where cannibalization is inevitable, but you just want to minimize the damage that you do.

Let's say you are promoting a product that's particularly relevant during Halloween. You need to decide what pages of your website to promote it on. But promoting this product means less promotion for another product. So you might generate a list of all your pages and sort them by the amount of traffic that you had in October. You can see that pages A through E are the top quintile for traffic. That is, they are the top 20% of pages for page views. You can grab this data from Google Analytics and export it to Excel. We are particularly interested in the high traffic pages. That is because the pages with low traffic may not be worth the effort. Page Z, for example, might only be worth $100. So it's not even really worth changing. It might take $500 worth of your labor time just to bother with it.

Now you can see that pages C, CF and Z all fall within the bottom quintile for conversion rates. These are among the lowest converting pages. But since everything after F has low traffic. We're not really even going to consider them. What we're really interested in is what pages with high volume also happen to have low conversion rates. And based on this analysis, there was only one page that really applies. That is, See? By promoting the product on this page, we'll hopefully make a big impact on the business while making a small impact on cannibalization. We can run tests to see whether the conversion rate for the new product was higher than for the old product. We could also calculate the overall profit or revenue impact. To determine whether to do the same promotion for next Halloween.

Product life cycle decisions

Product life cycle. Marketing decisions will vary depending on where you are in the product life cycle. Here you can see the typical stages and sales curve that are used to depict the life cycle. A lot of thought. Leadership and marketing comes from people who manage products at the maturity stage.

Often these are consumer packaged goods products from companies such as Procter and Gamble. At this stage, there's a strong emphasis on competition and cost cutting to drive up profit margins. There is also a heavy emphasis on massive brand marketing campaigns. But as a product marketing manager, the context is often completely different. You'll likely be working with products at the introduction and growth phases at these stages. You often don't need to focus very much on competitors. That is because the market is growing and can support many different competitors.

Moreover, brand awareness may be so low. That customers just aren't aware that you even have competitors. Cost cutting may also be less important. One reason for this is that growth will come from other sources, such as expanding revenue and a growing market. Your target. In this case, early adopters are also often less price sensitive. So you can make up for high expenses with high prices. In these stages, massive brand marketing is also less relevant. You and your competitors probably haven't built up the economies of scale that are required to invest in TV campaigns. There are few other points I want to make about strategy in the early stages of a product. It is sometimes difficult to have a strategy.

The product may change rapidly to accommodate whatever market signals you receive. You don't have a lot of data on customers and it's difficult to find what your target market really is. And your value proposition may not even be all that different from your competitors. I'm a huge fan of strategy, but I must admit that in the early stages, trial and error can sometimes be more important than strategic planning.

How Brands Grow - Part 1

In this chapter, I'm going to talk about some groundbreaking research that comes from Byron Sharp in his books on how brands grow. One of the biggest things that we learn from Byron Sharp is that conventional marketing wisdom, the mainstream thinking and marketing is actually very wrong in many different ways. Now, my personal thought is conventional marketing wisdom, which often comes from Philip Cutler, who is an expert in professional services marketing.

I think it is true and it holds true when you're trying to do something like a market, a small marketing agency or some small professional services firm. However, when you get into product marketing and you get into scaling up these things that are generally held as true or actually quite wrong, and we're going to steer you in the wrong direction. So what are these commonly held beliefs? Well, the first is that you should focus on retention because acquisition is supposedly more expensive. But Byron Sharp tells us that acquisition is actually the key to growth. That's what you should be focusing on.

And one of the reasons is that things like loyalty programs generally don't work. And loyalty is to some extent outside of your control. So your best chances at growth are really getting more people to buy your product. Rather than focusing on retaining your existing customer base. Now, a second widely held belief in the marketing world is that you need to appeal to a narrow group of target customers. Essentially the essence of target marketing, if you will. But what Byron Sharp shows us using a lot of data analysis is that really what you should be doing is targeting all category buyers and that this is the key to scaling up.

This is going to go against. Some really strongly held beliefs, perhaps among some of the people listening to this if you've done marketing for a long time. But if you look at certain types of advertising that's designed to get reach through things like Facebook or LinkedIn ads, you realize it's actually pretty cost effective to target all category buyers. It's not super expensive. It may be inefficient in some ways, but the benefits of scale will probably outweigh the inefficiency. Now, a third commonly held belief in the marketing world is that you need to communicate what makes you better or different.

So this is the obsession in product marketing around positioning basically. So finding that one little thing to focus on highlighting that in your marketing communications, really trying to communicate in a rational way to buyers. Why? Why you're different, why you're better. But what Byron Sharp tells us is that really what you should be focusing on is not how fundamentally you are different from competitors, but more how are you superficially different? And he uses the word distinctive. So these are things like, do you have a particular mascot that's identified with your brand or a particularly strong logo? So it's more about superficial differences rather than fundamental differences.

One of the reasons for this is that customers often have similar needs regardless of whether they're your customers or competitors' customers. So talking about why you're different may actually just give people a reason not to buy from you. And if you're trying to scale up, you need to appeal to a broad set of customers. Now, I'm going to add my own thoughts on this, which is that most businesses at the top of their game have competitors that offer pretty much the same thing. Now sometimes I run across these marketing gurus on LinkedIn and YouTube, etc., and they say, Oh, you really need to talk about how you're different. You need to own some sort of unique position.

But in reality, that's just not true. Highly successful companies have competitors that offer more or less the same product. So, for example, in the business consumer world, we have Coke and Pepsi, which are really not that different, fundamentally the same product. And then Coke comes out with a sugar free product. Pepsi does the same thing. Then they come up with Coke zero, Pepsi comes up with Pepsi zero. So these companies are hugely successful, even though they're pretty much just doing what their competitors are doing. Is that wrong? No, it's actually one of the ways to maintain your market share, grow your market share and maintain your profitability. And in the business to business world, even in professional services, we look at McKinsey and Bain.

Are they fundamentally different? Well, you might pretend that there are differences, but really, McKinsey, Bain, Boston Consulting Group, they're offering pretty much the same thing to the same set of customers. So this emphasis on differentiation is highly overrated, especially in the product marketing world. So having a unique position is not really your end goal, despite a lot of widely held beliefs in this regard. What you're really trying to achieve is economies of scale so that you become part of an oligopoly that competes with products that are largely the same as yours.

Market share is the most important factor when you're doing product marketing. It's not really about having some ultra special, unique position, some blue ocean strategy. I think this steers people in the wrong direction, especially for those that are highly ambitious. And one of the reasons that I really resonate with the research of Byron Sharp is because it's consistent with my experience where a lot of my key business financial success came from, going after broader audiences, going with kind of all in one solutions that I market it to customers, and that's been highly lucrative to me. The other thing is that I put a lot of faith in Bruce Greenwald and the research that you find in his book Competition Demystified. So Bruce Greenwald is looking at value investors like Warren Buffett and trying to analyze how they choose profitable businesses to invest in. And it's those that have a moat.

And the most powerful moat that you can have is economies of scale. So the strongest competitive advantage, the most sustainable one, is going to be economies of scale. So really, from a marketing perspective, that means achieving market share. And you don't really achieve huge market share with narrow targeting and narrow positioning. You have to have broader appeal and you have to have broader targeting. So that's very consistent with some of what Byron Sharp is saying about why conventional marketing wisdom just doesn't work.

7 Rules for Brand Growth

I'm going to talk about the seven rules for brand growth that come from Byron Sharp. The reason I want to elaborate on these is because they're based on empirical evidence. So this is not just guesswork or marketing stuff that's been made up by a marketing guru. And then what I'm going to do is give specific examples of my own to demonstrate each of these rules. So, number one, continuously reach all buyers of the category. An example of this in B to C would be targeting everyone that has an interest in a specific topic on Facebook.

This might give you the capability of reaching millions of people instead of simply hundreds or thousands. Rather than getting very granular and saying, well, I only want to hit certain segments of that or people that meet certain demographic variables. Instead you just sort of blanket hit all of those people that have a specific interest. Similarly in business to business, you might target everyone in a specific industry using LinkedIn ads, using something like a video ad where you're optimizing for reach and awareness rather than limiting yourself to those who simply submit a form or do some sort of lead gen activity number to ensure the brand is easy to buy. So an example of this would be doing search engine optimization so that when somebody is ready to buy yours they're very capable of finding your specific brand, your specific product.

Another thing is to have different payment options. So a high entry price or an onboarding price for your product might be a barrier for people to buy. So giving people more options might be helpful. Get noticed. An example of this would be doing an attention grabbing video on YouTube. So people are constantly being bombarded with advertising messages, with marketing messages. So something that's very attention grabbing, maybe like an explosion at the beginning of the video would be one way of getting noticed. Refresh and rebuild memory structures. So a lot of what makes good marketing is really about mental availability.

So conquering the mind space of potential buyers so that you're more prominent there in specific buying situations than your competitors are. So one way you would do this is in your creative and your advertisements in particular, you want to associate your product with a specific buying situation or a buyer, and Sharp would call a category entry point. So this might be something like breakfast. Oh, it's breakfast. What kind of brands come to mind? What products come to mind to satisfy myself at breakfast time or in business to business, it might be something like incorporation in corporations happened. Maybe there's a certain place I go to consider filling out legal forms or something like that.

Number five: Create and use distinctive brand assets. An example of this would be the mascot that Salesforce uses. They're not simply relying on the standard colors or the standard images. They're not using the psychology of color that all of their competitors perhaps would use. Instead, they're using something that's very bold, it's very different, that's very distinctive, and that is their mascot. And there's probably nothing that can more differentiate yourself in terms of brand distinctiveness than a mascot or spokesperson or some sort of face. Number six, be consistent. A lot of advertising agencies out there are trying to revise things, do rebranding, and come up with new ideas. But often what's most effective is having the same logo, the same mascot, the same colors, and in a lot of cases using the exact same creative.

Maybe modifying it to some extent, revising it with more modern situations, but fundamentally being consistent because people may not notice you except periodically during the year. So they're easily going to get confused if you start changing things up. You internally in your company may be sick of the same logo, the same colors, the same creative, but the consumer or the customer probably isn't. They simply don't think of you enough. So consistency is going to help them recall you.

And lastly, number seven, stay competitive, for example, the compelling options that your competitors are also offering. So if your competitors introduce something like sugar free, then that's something that you probably want to consider. Or if your competitors start offering something like unlimited support, you probably want to offer that as well. Another aspect of this that I would highlight is share of choice. So if your competitors have a very strong share of voice, you probably want to invest at least as much as your competitors are, possibly even focusing on excess, excess share of voice to make sure that you're able to grow your market share rather than simply maintain it.

Marketing Laws

Similar to the laws of physics. We also have laws of marketing, which Byron Sharp gives us, and there are few of these that I would like to call out. The first is double jeopardy, which essentially says that small brands have fewer buyers who are less loyal. So this goes against the mindset of niche positioning, blue ocean strategies. Often we're told that if we just find some particular niche and find the perfect target customer group, that they're going to love us. They're going to fall in love with us and maintain loyalty with us. But that's really not true.

Even in cases where there's particularly high customer satisfaction scores or NPS scores, people are less loyal to those products, to those brands, to those companies, because what dictates loyalty is not so much satisfaction or falling in love with the brand. It has more to do with convenience and things like mental and physical availability. So this reasserts the importance of achieving high market share rather than trying to be a small, niche brand. Second law here is the law of buyer moderation, which says that heavy buyers become light buyers and light buyers become heavy buyers and buyers will enter and exit the category. So for example, they will become non buyers when they die or when they simply change their diets or they change their needs, they change companies.

So there's this state of flux that's happening, which basically is a regression to the mean over time and over a wide customer base. So the idea that you can just target the heavy users and focus on them strategically would be somewhat a contradiction of the law of buyer moderation. Third law we have is the duplication of purchase, which is that all brands within a category share their customer base with other brands in proportion to their size, which again highlights the importance of scale and achieving market share. So in a category, chances are that you're going to compete more with the big brands in your category than the other small players that perhaps look more like you.

Lastly, we have the law of prototypical cities and this direct quotation is image attributes that describe the product category score higher, i.e. are more commonly associated with a brand than less prototypical attributes. So this contradicts the idea that you should have some sort of unique positioning, that you should emphasize your points of difference. In a lot of cases, you're going to have the most success when you're simply highlighting attributes that are typical of your category. So taking a broader positioning or a more generic positioning or a less differentiated positioning is going to be successful in terms of achieving mental availability.

Differentiation vs Distinctiveness

Differentiation vs Distinctiveness is a heated marketing debate. My answer may offend some marketers because it uproots some tightly held beliefs. If you disagree with me, feel free to message me so I can explain. Differentiation refers to substantive differences between products or value propositions while distinctiveness refers to superficial distinctions such as branded design elements. Differentiation just doesN'T matter for the vast majority of products. This is clear from research at the Kellogg School of Management and the Ehrenberg-Bass Institute. It applies to both B2B & B2C.

It's also clear from the market's surprising appetite for redundancy. Consider, for example, all the similar luxury products under the LVMH umbrella and their near-identical competitors who deviate on superficial grounds such as with patterns or logos. Consider all the "me-too" product variations on Amazon. The real world doesn't value uniqueness as much as marketers think it does.

Buyers have fairly preset/fixed ideas about what they want and won't buy things that deviate far from those expectations. Consider that most record-breaking movies are just retelling the same old predictable stories from previous movies. Typically they mimic 9/10 standard movie expectations with 1 change. Avator, for example, is recycling the same story as Dances with Wolves/Pocahontas/The Last Samurai only the setting is changed to an alien planet. Consider all the fast-food burger joints that continue to thrive despite strong incumbents like McDonald's and Burger King. Or consider the "me-too" product offerings on Amazon. Uniqueness wins awards but is NOT the sure-fire path to revenue.

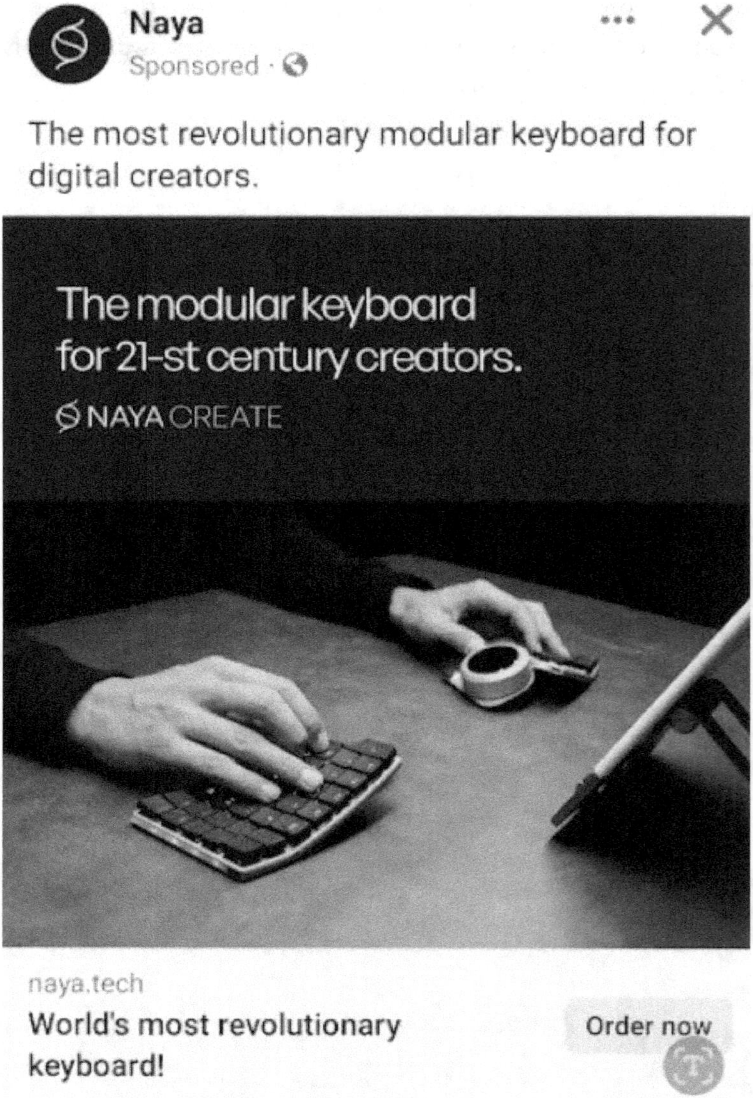
Naya
Sponsored ·
The most revolutionary modular keyboard for digital creators.
The modular keyboard
for 21-st century creators.
NAYA CREATE
naya.tech
World's most revolutionary keyboard!
Order now

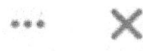

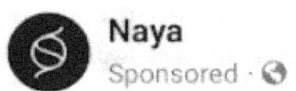

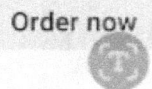

Above is an example of a differentiated product—one that is attempting to avoid the "red ocean" of competition for standard keyboards. But if you look at the first page of top-selling keyboards on Amazon, you'll notice that not a single one looks like this. Companies large & small both win when they compete for visibility rather than uniqueness. Product marketers spend too much time trying to avoid competition through positioning rather than trying to gain as much visibility as possible.

The recipe for success is to give the market what it already wants...in other words, meet the demand rather than try to create demand for something new. Yes, sometimes creating a new product category with a unique innovation is successful. But this is the exception, not the rule. In this Book, I do teach you how to craft intricate value propositions for unique products, but you have to recognize that these are minority situations. Differentiation often produces products or benefits with NO demand. Below it's clear that people want light, gray-and-black vests with horizontal divisions. What matters is familiarity, visibility & distinctive brand assets.

Undifferentiated but distinctive
products often produce more sales

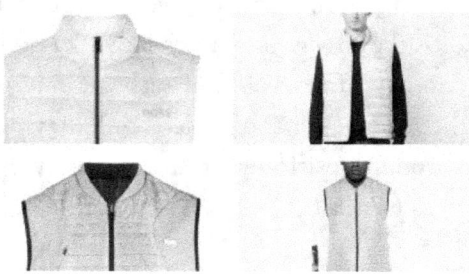

Despite this clarity, most product marketers operate under the false assumption that their product needs to be positioned uniquely. BUT there are important exceptions for some highly involved purchases such as:

(1) A minority of B2B products that are "strategic purchases"

(2) Most professional services

By default, assume that your product should be positioned the same as competitors in your product category. For example, you might fare better with positioning around "live chat plugin" rather than discussing how your chat plugin is different or how it generates more revenue than competitors. You go through a more involved positioning exercise only when you find a special reason to do so (e.g., it's clear that you're selling a strategic purchase that will be evaluated extensively on the basis of ROI.) In most situations, you don't compete by being different, but rather, by being more visible: e.g., more shelf space, more visible in search engines, more awareness ads, more mind share. The best product doesn't win as much as the most well known one.

Examples of superficial distinctiveness: McDonald's golden arches, Tiffany's color, Tony the Tiger, Salesforce's cute mascot, Rimowa's grooves, handbags with different patterns that do not affect functionality. Examples of substantive differentiation: holographic keyboard vs mechanical keyboard, marketing firm that only does LinkedIn ads vs a generic marketing agency.

Nike Example: Big Product Marketing Mistake

In this Nike case study. What I'm going to demonstrate is one of the most common mistakes that people make in product marketing. And that mistake is hyper focusing on narrow targeting. So product marketers often believe that the primary goal of their job is to identify some special little niche group of people to appeal to, to target, and to make them fall in love with your product. In reality, that's not generally how you grow.

The way that you generally grow is by targeting larger clusters of customers. And often what that means is targeting all people who buy the product category. So in the case of Nike, that product category generally is sports apparel. Now let's take a look at this example. So these are two products that I own. On the left, we have a shirt, a dry fit shirt that keeps you dry when you're running. And you can see that it falls under the Sub Brand Nike running division. And you can see that in the logo. Here on the right, we have a jacket and the jacket falls under a different sub brand, which is basically the Nike lifestyle brand.

Now, you'll notice a big difference between the logos here on the right, we have the Nike check mark with the written words Nike. Now, the reason that it is this way is because this lifestyle product is designed to have a retro feel. So it's bringing you back to some of the classic Nike clothing. And back then, Nike wasn't as well known and associated with the check mark. So often what you have to do is a newer brand or a smaller brand to really solidify the connection between the icon, i.e. the check mark in this case and the brand name. So Nike, so that eventually the check mark itself will be sufficient to make people think of the brand name Nike. But back then that solidification hadn't happened yet.

However, they're still branding their lifestyle products with this to give it a retro feel. So really what we're doing here is we're targeting different use cases. So the use case for this jacket is lifestyle. It's fashion. It's casually going out and on the left it's much more functional. It's about running and the technical capabilities of the shirt itself to keep you dry, to keep you cool, etc.. Whereas on the right, it's not so much about functionality, it's more about how cool or how fashionable you are. Very, very different use cases. So the tendency with product marketers and product marketing managers when they're first getting started is they would look at this and they would say, Well, Nike running division products, these performance products, we're going to target people that are running competitively, people that are only interested in running.

And then we're going to have this completely separate group of people that are only interested in fashion and really aren't into sports and reality. Those two use cases overlap, and I'm the perfect demonstration of that. I want to wear Nike lifestyle products, but I also, because I do a lot of running, want to wear functional products. It doesn't mean that I'm a different group or I'm a different target or a different subsegment of the target customer group Nike's targeting. It's that I am the same person, but with different needs. So this is an inversion of how you need to think of targeting. When you're doing product marketing, are you actually targeting different people or are you targeting the same people with different use cases?

And we see this all the time in the business world. So, for example, Coca Cola sells Diet Coke, which has zero calories, and they also sell regular Coke, which has a lot of calories. And you might think, oh, there's a diet segment, there's people that only drink diet soda. No, there are people that drink diet soda during the week. And then on the weekends when they want a treat, they'll have the full sugar version of Coca Cola.

Now, it's very easy to get caught up in this belief because this is the mainstream thinking in marketing, largely based on what's coming out of academia, this idea of hyper targeting. But when we actually look at consumer behavior, we see that in fact the same people will buy different products for different reasons, for different use cases. So it's not so much a targeting issue as a use case or value proposition issue.

AI in Product Marketing is Nothing New

I And marketing is really nothing new. I know an expert who has basically been doing nothing for the last ten years other than using artificial intelligence to help with customer acquisition marketing for a major telecom provider. Eight years ago I was using different AI techniques and tools like Microsoft Azure to do things like make predictions and marketing and to segment customer bases. What's different is that ten years ago, a more popular term was used and it's called machine learning.

Now AI is a popular term. So really what's happened is we've undergone a rebranding, a superficial rebranding of what we now call artificial intelligence or AI. So it's just rebranding an old idea. Now I'm going to give you three examples of where AI has already had a huge contribution to the marketing world. The first is cluster analysis. Now usually when marketers want to segment the market, what they do is they make arbitrary decisions. We're going to segment by male and female, we're going to segment by the size of the company.

We're going to make guesses at how we're going to split up customer bases. But cluster analysis is using artificial intelligence where we input tons of data. So for example, 2000 survey responses on 20 different questions and we say, okay, I tell us what the market segments are, and then we can look at a graph and we can see clearly that there are around maybe five major segments and they cluster around different variables. So for example, maybe it's people that travel a lot. They also happen to be in their 30s and they suffer a particular pain point and that cluster has been created with artificial intelligence because humans are actually really bad with dealing with large datasets, looking at things that are overly complex. AI does a good job of doing that.

Cluster analysis does a good job of doing that. So the first example is segmentation. The second example is something we call RFM. So RFM is a model that marketers have used to predict who is most likely to respond to something like a direct mail letter. And what RFM stands for is frequency and monetary value. But now we don't need to rely on RFM. We can rely on something more sophisticated, which is artificial intelligence, predictive analytics. Now the third example is using AI to make other predictions. And one good example of this is when we're trying to predict what product customers will likely buy next so that we can push that product to them, whether it's through email, direct mail or an advertisement.

So this is what we call a next product buy prediction, and artificial intelligence is how we do that. So marketers have been using AI for a long time. They often just called it machine learning. But the key challenge was that it was generally most useful with large companies because large companies could afford the tools, the upgrades, the AI upgrades and Salesforce, for example, or the advanced statistical equipment that you needed to analyze, and also just the large datasets. If you had a large number of customers, a large number of survey responses, then you could use AI effectively.

So it wasn't as useful for small businesses that are more agile and just can't afford these capabilities. Now we have tools like ChatGPT, which is free, that empower small companies to be able to use AI in their marketing.